WHAT O
ABC

"Sheila is one of the most talented intuitives I have met. She has the incredible ability to simplify complex information. When she shared with me the energies regarding astrology and the Moon, and the meaning behind their symbols, I applied the information and wow—the results were amazing. As an example, during the month of May, I learned from Sheila that the energy of Taurus was powerful in that desires for the coming month may be met through staying focused and using the power of Taurus to manifest one's heart's desire.

"I listened intently to Sheila as she described how to best use the energy to serve self and others. It was the strangest thing: as I was leaving her home, I was centered with such peace and well-being that my drive home was effortless, and I did not encounter one red traffic light, which is extremely unusual in my community. Throughout the month, I reminded myself of Sheila's wisdom and, though I encountered a few challenges, my desires were fulfilled so much so that I was given a new car—something I had wanted for several years. I believe Sheila can certainly help one understand how to recognize the energies and manifest that which is in our highest good as an individual and as a global community.."

— Gena, NEWS RADIO 970AM K-NEWS, Las Vegas, NV

"Sheila Stirling uses her love for others and her powerful intuition to bring us the gift of reading the language of the cosmos. As Sheila states: 'We and everything in the universe are moving through a complex sea of energy. While the currents in that sea are constantly changing, they are predictable. Using this book as a guide allows us to move through this energy in the direction of these flows instead of against them.' In the Stirling Formula, Sheila has taken very complex esoteric concepts and created an elegantly simple way to apply this ancient knowledge, so everyone can use this material. Brilliant work, Sheila."

— Elissa MacLachlan, Ph.D., Mh.D., psycho-spiritual counselor [www.spiritleap.com/index.html]

"I see Shelia as a devout student of the universe and a transmitter of the wisdom and the energies of the stars. Perhaps, due to my having read Sheila's book, *Reading the Language of the Cosmos*, I have paid particular attention this year to the history of the Magi ... the three Wise Men from the east who followed the Star announcing the birth of the Christ child. I have learned that these three were highly respected for their knowledge of the stars and what they knew of Old Testament scriptures. It was because of their knowledge that they recognized the appearance of an unusual star with unusual energy—what we call the Bethlehem Star. They set out on foot to find this promised event and they walked a distance equivalent to the distance between Las Vegas and Salt Lake City to be with this divine child. It is truly said that wise men (women) still seek these divine mysteries. I believe, whether Shelia realizes it or not, she has been embraced by the divine—He that reveals to her the great wisdom, the eternal truths from which we all can benefit. "Knock and it shall be opened ... seek and you will find." Thanks, Shelia, for being such a beautiful transmitter! I love you, Shelia. Keep on reaching for and reading the stars!"

— Lillian Jennings, CRS, CCIM

"This is not just another astrology book but an inspired and highly specialized treatise on KABBALASTROLOGY in which Sheila Z has integrated Sun and Moon, Macrocosm and Microcosm into a useful guide for daily living. Illustrating cosmic forces with personal insights and concrete examples, this book offers each of us insight into how these forces affect our lives, enabling us to utilize them as constructive tools for personal growth while avoiding pitfalls that plague the unwary. Let this book be a Light on your path!"

— Star Cravingmad, Magician and Astrologer

Reading the Language of the Cosmos

2009 Edition

Your astrological energy almanac with
ancient celebrations and remembrances

...

2009 daily moon signs and energy
calendar with moon phases

...

2009 retrograde chart

Sheila Z. Stirling

Reading the Language of the Cosmos
by Sheila Z. Stirling

Copyright © 2004 – 2008 Sheila Z. Stirling

ISBN 978-0-9778891-4-3

2009 edition November, 2008

Published by
Wisdom Press
4132 S. Rainbow Blvd. #465,
Las Vegas NV, 89103
Web site: www.OpenWisdomInstitute.com

Contents of this book are copyrighted. No part may be reproduced by mechanical means, photocopy or computer without written authorization of the publisher (except for brief quotations by reviewers).

Note from the author and publisher: The information in this book is not meant in any way to diagnose or replace medical advice or treatment.

To order more copies of this book, please call toll-free: 1-866-612-7051, or order online at:
www.OpenWisdomInstitute.com

Edited and designed by Tony Stubbs, www.tjpublish.com

Cover design by Katlyn Breene

Printed in the United States of America

Table of Contents

Acknowledgments vi
Dedication viii
Preface x
Introduction xi
The Effects of the Moon xiii
Etheric Energy xv
Origin of the Stirling Formula xvi
Using the Stirling Formula xviii
Why Kabbalah? xxi
About the Hebrew Letters xxiii
How to Use the Galactic Guide xxiv
The Time of Aries 1
The Time of Taurus 5
The Time of Gemini 11
The Time of Cancer 15
The Time of Leo 21
The Time of Virgo 27
The Time of Libra 33
The Time of Scorpio 37
The Time of Sagittarius 41
The Time of Capricorn 45
The Time of Aquarius 49
The Time of Pisces 55
Epilogue 59
Glossary 60
Planets 61
The Seasons and Celebrations 64
Ancient Remembrances 66
Moon Sign Charts for 2009 68
Planetary Energy for 2009: Retrograde and Direct Positions 84
About the Author 81
Notes 86
CDs, Books, etc. 94

ACKNOWLEDGEMENTS

I would like to thank Divine Spirit for taking me in, for caressing me and for sharing some profound wisdom with me.

I am so grateful to so many wonderful people in my life who accept me for whom I am and smile upon me. My wonderful daughter, Shane, and my awesome grandsons, Sage and Elijah, and now a new granddaughter Sierra, who are always an inspiration of love manifest for me. It is so amazing to watch from year to year as they blossom and bloom. My sister Joy, who cares deeply, and is a catalyst for me. My mom who, even in her waning days, saw the beauty in every sunrise and the majesty in all of nature. My inner circle of close friends, who encourage and inspire me, and my spirit family who WOW me with their love and kindness. And the many who have gone on before us. I thank you for being in my world and encouraging me always.

Thank you, Tony Stubbs, for being the most patient editor and helping to bring this writing into this reality. And Lynne Palmer for wanting my book to be perfect and going over every word with the highest of intention. You are world renown for your expertise in the astrology field.

And I am thankful for the ancient ways, the Book of Formation that was handed down from Abraham the great some 4,000 years ago, yes, it is still the technology of the light. And to my Sonny Bear, whose spirit sits beside me, loves me and comforts me always.

I give thanks for the creative magic that lives in the heart of Katlyn Breene, the cover artist, and I am thankful and grateful for the Ancient Ones, out in the Cosmos who beamed this information directly into my being.

I am thankful for you who picked up this writing and felt the value in knowing this wisdom. To know the energy of each day and how it will be affecting each one of us.

I wish you the brightest of blessings and the kindest of thoughts. Thank you, thank you. I am forever grateful for you.

In service,

Sheila Z. Stirling

Dedication

I would like to honor the memory of my mother, Pearl, who lived the life of a true artist, seeing the beauty in nature and in all around her. Her love of my self-expression and her willingness to believe in anything and everything I chose to do made her an integral part of my life. For always being there for me, and for being such a positive force, I honor you.

This sharing is dedicated to the process of our evolution, to the conscious spiritual evolution of all. May it encourage people to open the channels to better communication, and lead to an understanding of the energies that surround our world. May we seek to work with the energies that influence our lives from moment to moment.

SZS

"A human being is a part of the whole, called by us 'Universe,' a part limited in time and space.

He experiences himself, his thoughts and feelings as something separated from the rest - a kind of optical delusion of his consciousness.

This delusion is a kind of prison for us, restricting us to our personal desires and to affection for a few persons nearest to us.

Our task must be to free ourselves from this prison by widening our circle of compassion to embrace all living creatures and the whole of nature in its beauty.

The striving for such achievement is in itself a part of the liberation and a foundation for innersecurity."

— Albert Einstein

Preface

What if one day you realized that everything you had learned and believed up to this point was not correct, although it had brought you to where you are now, knowing that everything is really as one, and that it is energy that connects the All, and that the All is energy displayed as millions of variations and vibrations in the time space signature?

What if the vast distance between the planets and the constellations was not just empty space but rather waves upon waves of information carried by the energy within the energy, meant to guide you and open you to the coming evolution of our species?.

What if you woke up one day and could see this information as a language, and the language flowed into your mind and into your heart, and you suddenly realized it is part of the interpretation of the wisdom of the ages?

What if you could read the Language of the Cosmos like so many letters on a page?

This is exactly what happened to me, and why I wrote this book.

Introduction

In the beginning, there was nothingness; then there was the light. The heavens sparkled with the mystery of the stars that man longed to unlock. Since the dawn of humanity, seers have gazed up at the starry skies and known with certainty that the planets and the constellations have a profound effect on all life.

The study of the stars, the Sun and the Moon is part of every culture. Countless volumes have been written about the ebb and flow of our tides and the effect this holds for all beings. Some of the world's oldest and wisest texts have been written on the Zodiac, while each day millions of people throughout the world check their horoscope before venturing outside.

The constellations mark the rotation of our Earth. There is the Earth, the sky, oceans, sun and moon, the elements of air, water, fire and earth. The lunar follows the solar that follows the lunar in an endless circle as they dance across our night sky. With this rotation comes a circle of knowing and wisdom, the answer that awaits the gazer who asks, "What does all this mean?"

Each month, the shifting planets and their constellations pour down powerful forces upon our minds and our emotions. We cannot see or hear these forces, yet they are so compelling that they shape events on a global level. This book examines the astral forces that come in waves of energy, and their effect on us all. This book gives an in-depth interpretation of the energies I define as the "language of the cosmos."

It is amazing to realize that we are all a part of the astral energies. Everyone and everything really is connected. Deep inside, we all know that energy is really everything, be it life, fulfillment, trees, or rocks. We know that energy is all around us, within us and that we are one with it. The concept is easily stated, but when we really take it into our hearts and souls, that is something altogether different.

The Cosmos beckons us to seek the wisdom of this language, to translate it and incorporate it into our everyday lives for our betterment and highest good. By understanding this language, we can only enhance the quality of our lives.

Einstein believed that everything is energy. As he said, "Nothing happens until something moves." Thus our every thought has an effect on energy, and vice versa. Every thought affects the energy everywhere, like a drop of water creating a ripple throughout the universe.

This is so important I will say it again: *Every thought affects the energy everywhere.* As we speak the thought, it becomes manifest, which gave us the saying: "Be careful what you wish for because you might just get it." What we put our energy into does manifest. The trick is to be able to consciously put our most wonderful and highest thoughts forward, rather than some doubtful thoughts that may be lurking underneath.

My epiphany came when I realized that each and every day, we are genuinely affected by the energies of the planets and constellations. By knowing the astral energies on a daily basis and understanding how this interaction affects each of us, we can put our understanding to good use. Using the techniques in this book, we can make the minor adjustments that will bring more joy and fulfillment into your life and the life of those around you. This book is about getting out of our own story enough to understand our relationship and interaction with the Cosmos. This is not a book you read once and put away. Keep it on your nightstand, take it with you on trips, consult it often and be prepared for your life.

The Effects of the Moon (Daily and Monthly)

As the Moon makes her* 28-day orbit around the Earth, she travels through the constellations that make up the 12 Signs of the Zodiac. As this occurs, the energy of both the Moon and zodiac sign are accentuated and the reflective information comes to Earth on waves of energy. The sign's energy is reflected and filtered through the Moon's energy and affects each being, moment-to-moment.

The Moon, or Luna, has an astounding effect on all water on this planet, including the ebb and flow of the tides. So it makes perfect sense that we as humans, made up of 50 – 80 % water, are affected in a profound way as well.

To pass through all signs in 27¼ days, the moon occupies each sign for between 48 and 52 hours. If I know that tomorrow the moon will be crossing Taurus, then I know there will be obstacles that day that may distract me from my goal. But I also know it is persistence and keeping my eye on the goal that will carry me through that day. I will also be challenged with self-doubt and matters of the heart. So having a heads' up on this energy will allow me to be proactive and not reactive. Armed with this knowledge, I will be assured that all will be fine and not give in to doubt. I will be able to act with love, compassion and kindness for myself as well as others, and will know this energy will soon give way to the influence of Gemini.

---

* I refer to the Moon as feminine in the sense of being reflective and deep. In the ancient ways, the Moon is referenced as feminine as the Sun is masculine, the Moon as the great mother and nurturer, with the Sun as the strong and powerful male king.

There is also a factor in astral energies called 'void of course.' This is when the Moon is traveling and there is a gap of earth time when there is no reflective energy coming from a specific planet or sign. It only lasts a few hours, but it's as if the cosmos is taking a deep breath before entering the next energy flow. We may think of this as a time of reprieve, when we're free of all influences of the cosmos. My intuition and channeling tell me there is great meaning in this time. For as in meditation and many healing modalities, it is the gap between the thoughts that can cause spontaneous healings. This place of nothingness may, in fact, be the place where the All resides. And so in these precious few hours, I feel our human potential and possibilities become boundaryless, as they always are and always have been. When the Moon is Void of Course, it is a wonderful time to wind up and finish projects you have started.

Etheric Energy

Are the energies the same for everyone? The answer is YES, the incoming energies are constant. It is the same energy however the individual interpretation of the energy is where the similarity ends.

Why is this such an individual interpretation? That is a great question and the answer may seem simple but it is interwoven into the very fabric of our being. The word 'etheric' comes from the word *ether*. The Etheric Body is also sometimes called our energy field. If you are alive, you have an energy field. Plants and animals, minerals and most everything on this planet carries an energy signature. It is all around us. As the waves of information travel through what looks like empty space and this energy hits an energy signature or etheric field of a person, each person, being so unique and infinitely wondrous, will feel the energy in a different way. In other words, our bodies interpret this energy on a cellular level and in a very unique way, a way that reflects our own personal experiences, past and present. How we come and go through this life, how we feel and think, patterns both learned and inherit, all come into play. So no two people will usually feel the exact same thing at the exact same time. This is all part of the evolutionary leap we are experiencing now here on Mother Earth.

Origin of the Stirling Formula
How did I think of this? Where did it come from?

There is a very long story that goes with this question, but for now, here is the short version. Basically I was in a very bad automobile accident late in 1999, when I sustained head trauma injuries among others, and suddenly found myself in other realms, spending time with angels and receiving messages and whole thought forms and concepts from beyond. After trying to convince myself, "I am not a channel," I had no choice but to accept that, "Yes I am a channel and yes, I do receive information from what I believe to be the infinite one, God, Source, the galaxy, the beyond, or whatever you choose to call it." I further now know we are all channels, and it just depends what frequencies we are tuned to. So, with that in mind, here's what happened.

One evening as I was sitting in my meditation room, a chill came over and through me. I knew from experience that some information was about to come through me, placed into my heart and my mind. I took a deep breath and relaxed into my large, soft chair. I received an awakening, an 'Ah ha,' when all the years of studying so many different energy concepts and ancient technologies came together right in front of me. I knew the Cosmos was speaking to me, directly to me. I could see it and understand it, and in that moment, the Stirling Formula was born. Literally, letters began to fall from out of nowhere and colorful waves upon waves of information were downloaded directly into my being. It felt as if someone were trying to fill an empty cup! I was becoming full and started to panic: *How am I going to remember all of this and write it down?*

After a time, the information subsided and I quickly ran to my computer and began to put down in words what had been shown to me, to be used to help the evolution of our humanness. We are becoming universal beings. I know we have always been that, but now we are beginning to remember and open to what lies beyond our wildest dreams.

My philosophy includes the belief that each of us carries the source of creation within. Life is a spiritual adventure to be explored and shared. An internal light shines within us all. As we develop our universal skills and hear the call of the Ancient Ones, we become anchors for the new millennium. Our human evolution is reaching out for our soul's purpose, and we need to clearly understand the potential that is within each of us.

Using the Stirling Formula

Using the Stirling Formula has had a profound and positive effect on my life, and I know as the book unfolds and the formula is revealed, it will have a profoundly positive effect in your life, as well.

I KNOW WITH CERTAINTY that: *We* are the ones who will carry this humanity into and beyond the 2012 energy, and that we truly possess the tools for enlightenment within us. The time is now to access our inner guidance and step out into the expanded cosmos of conscious evolution. We are poised to discover and experience love of self, the love and gratitude of Source, to achieve a higher level of consciousness, walk the walk of our divine selves, and promote health and healing for the betterment of our world and the future of this planet. We can live each day to create the reality we so desire. Every moment, we are being given the opportunity to better connect to the light and spirit we truly are.

I believe we are in a time of an evolutionary leap. We have an opportunity as never before to secure the future of this planet by using this blueprint to bring more light and energy into our own lives and into the world around us. With this understanding and gratitude for All That Is and feeling the blessings, we enter the world of the transformative soul. We see and understand that we are all here to learn and share our lightness and that this light will shine the way to peace, prosperity and fulfillment.

As you use the formula, you will see that no two months are alike. Each carries a unique signature and by understanding that signature, we gain the knowledge and the wisdom to work with these astral energies. Like pieces in a great puzzle, the more we can connect the pieces, the clearer the picture will become.

Throughout history, these energies have played an enormous role in global events. Unknowingly, people reacted to these influences like pawns on a great chessboard, without ever knowing or realizing that there is a divine order to these energies. It is my hope that, with greater understanding of these forces, we may begin to live in a gentler and more proactive way. Individually, this will lift our vibration of consciousness and will, in turn, affect everything in our world and the world around us.

The Stirling Formula combines ancient teachings, and provides an elegant pathway that will empower you and enable you to live a more proactive and fulfilling life. The Stirling Formula will help you to deal with these astral energies on a daily basis. Having a 'heads up' at the beginning of each incoming month can help us to recognize challenges and opportunities as they unfold.

Recommendation

The pages that follow explore yet another aspect of the cosmic dance. Not a new aspect, but in fact. some of the oldest wisdom on this planet. This is the knowledge that the constellations rain down energy on us from above, waiting for us to realize the opportunities that await us from moment to moment. The language of the cosmos is the language of energy.

Please remember that energy is energy, and everything is energy. There is no good energy or bad energy, but just energy. As this energy enters our world and our etheric space, we then interpret this energy in the very cells of our being, and act or react in our own individual way. It is important to note that in all things there is a cosmic balance.

Like it or not, this energy beaming down from the planets rotating across our skies has a positive energy that is mirrored by shadow energy. Knowing and understanding the shadow side of this energy is as essential as understanding the light and positive side.

When you read about the monthly energies and explore the energies of each planet, the constellations and elements, a pattern will emerge. As you apply this monthly formula, your life will open and change for the better. Your inner sight, the voice that speaks to you from within, will become clearer. You will learn to decipher when the energies are speaking and when it is your inner voice. You will be able to determine when these outside energies are pushing you to react, so you will have clearer choices. And choices are a very good thing indeed!

In working with the Formula, my life has changed for the better, much has become easier and there is a definite flow to my activities. I have learned to recognize when the energies are influencing my choices. I gained the knowledge to act and not react to life's situations.

Each morning before getting out of bed, I call to the energies and offer gratitude for the opportunities that await me each day. You may wish to keep a daily or monthly journal to chart your actions and reactions relating to the incoming energies. Jot down a few feelings when you sense a strong energy surge and you realize "Ah ha!" That may be one of those moments. There are blank pages at the back of the book to do that. Be aware that you can be hit with a wave of reactionary energy and use the monthly formula to resist these forces. Again, remember it is not always about us.

Finally, please note that all cycles are lunar cycles, as they are in many ancient philosophies. It is the Moon filtering these energies that adjusts the frequency to a human vibration.

Why the Book of Formation? Why Kabbalah?

Did you know that for about 4000 years, Kabbalists have been meeting, often in secret, on the 'Dark Moon,' or the head of the new month, which some people call the New Moon. The Kabbalists call this time *Rosh Choidsh*, meaning the head of the month, when the incoming energies of the new month were discussed. Each month has a word and a Hebrew letter that coincides with the energy of the month. When we scan these letters, we gain the benefit and the light from the letters of each month. The energy and light enters the soul by way of the eyes, which gave us the saying, "Your eyes are the windows of the soul."

Kabbalah is a vast body of knowledge and wisdom, and an instruction manual for all mankind on how to better receive the light. The original writing, called the *Book of Formation*, was written over 4,000 years ago by Abraham the Great. The original text had only about 3,000 words and from this body of writing has come all the countless books on Kabbalah.

It demonstrates to us how the laws of the universe manifest themselves in our material world. It has been *only about 80 years* since the Kabbalah was translated into English and opened up to the world. Before that, unless you were over 40 or a rabbi, you could not peer upon its words. It is believed that just by scanning your eyes on this ancient text, you allow more light more connection in. (Remember, the eyes are the windows to the soul.)

The word *Kabbalah* translates as 'to receive'; it is a practice that enables us to better connect and receive light. When I first started learning from Kabbalah, I remember thinking:

This is so simple. I already know this. But just by hearing and scanning the words, my life became transformed. In the way of Kabbalah, everything is energy. Light, energy and the face of fulfillment are as one. Energy = light and fulfillment.

Kabbalah gives us insight into the essence of universal law. Kabbalah is a daily practice. *There are no real short cuts*, but there are a few key elements that, by knowing them, you can change *your* world for the better in an instant! *And* the world around you.

Kabbalah is for all mankind. It is not a religion but a technology. Technology, according to Webster's dictionary, means: "The application of science in either industry or commerce, and the methods and materials thus used." Thus, Kabbalah is the method and materials used in gaining connection and receiving more light. And 'technique' is defined as: "The systematic procedure by which a task is accomplished." The Kabbalah offers a formula that will help us to reorganize; there is a blessing in every encounter and in every happening. This makes Kabbalah a very empowering tool set forth for the enlightenment of all creation.

Every chapter of this writing references the Kabbalah, because I feel it is important to acknowledge this age-old legacy and its impact on my belief system. For these are the roots from which the tree has blossomed.

About the Hebrew Letters

At the start of each sign, you will see the Hebrew letter that represents that month. This is ancient text and it is said these letters existed before the time of Language. In the way of Kabbalah, these shapes and forms of the letters make up the DNA of all life on this earth and the creation of this planet. It is said the first letter is the building block of all that is, and the second letter represents creation itself. To scan or to look upon the letters is to receive the light of source. An example would be the first letter for Pisces is pronounced "Kuf" and carries the code of the planet. The second letter is pronounced "Gimmel" and carries the code of DNA of all that is. There are 22 letters in the hebrew alphabet and these letters are said to be the pathway to enlightenment. These letters are the seed of the soul. Look or scan each letter as the month comes into view, take a moment and meditate on the letters, hold a humble prayer in your heart for the highest good for all. This practice may be very healing and increase your vibratory rate which will lift you to the next level of consciousness.

How to Use This Galactic Guide:

There are five sub-headings in each Zodiac sign (the 5th house being that of creativity and emergence, but that is another book entirely):

1. The energies of the sign and its ruling planet
2. In the Way of Kabbalah
3. Life Example of the Month's Energy
4. Stirling Formula
5. Daily moon energies. Use this information to adjust your daily direction and pro-active behavior. To learn which Sign of the Zodiac the Moon is in each day of the month, see my website: www.openwisdominstitute.com and click on the page "Moon Signs."

Each sub-heading will bring us to a new level of understanding the waves of information raining down on us from the cosmos. Just think … this information has been out there, unseen and untranslated since the dawn of time. Now you have the opportunity to utilize this information for your highest good and the highest good of all humanity.

The Time of Aries
21 March – 20 April
First sign of the Zodiac
Element: Fire
Ruling Planet: Mars

ENERGIES OF ARIES:

"Arise, oh Aries, head held high."

The first sign of the Zodiac, Aries begins on the 21st of March each year and is symbolized by the constellation of the Ram. The Hebrew name for the month of Aries is NISSAN. Aries brings with it the aspects of a pioneering spirit, enthusiastic and bursting with energy. Aries rains down bravery and endless creative ideas. The energy of Aries is fiercely competitive and yet easily hurt. Aries may also compel us to be impatient and impulsive, concerned with the self, the 'I am.'

The element of fire brings in the energies of passion and action; this is also the element of purification and transformation. Aries is ruled by Mars, the red planet of fire with all its Yang energy. Mars has a male energy signature and moves us to action and desire. In ancient times, the planet Mars was called 'the warrior god,' so you can begin to see the power that this combination of astral energies brings.

The first day of Aries marks the Vernal or Spring equinox—an event of cosmic proportion. This is one of the two days when light and darkness balance. The cosmic balance. This is the day when you can place an egg on its end and it will stand due to the gravitational pull being equal and balanced. Each day from now on, we add one or two minutes of light to our day until the Summer Solstice in the sign of cancer.

In the Way of Kabbalah:

Aries is the first sign of the Zodiac and brings in the energies of the pioneer spirit. It is in this month we were given, some 4,000 years ago, *The Book of Formation*, the text of the Kabbalah. It is also the month Abraham the Great chose to transition beyond the veils.

This is a powerful month and signifies new beginnings. It is wise to note that sometimes Aries will have a challenge—finishing what you start. Aries can also give a sense of false security. What is driving you? Is it the desire to share? Or is it ego? Use those great horns of the ram to pierce new openings. So go forth with sincerity.

LIFE EXAMPLE OF ARIES ENERGY:

Have you ever had one of those days when you spring out of bed, excited to be alive and make this the first day of the rest of your life? After grooming yourself and telling yourself how wonderful today is going to be, you go to the kitchen and make yourself a quick bite to eat. After all, you feel almost in a hurry to greet the day. When you get to the office, you jump into the new project with great enthusiasm. All is going very well and then somebody suggests a 'better way' of handling the project. You jump into action, ready to defend your brilliant ideas. You have such passion when you tell your colleague, "You're oh so wrong! I know the best way!"

You're ready to make war over this and you stand firm in your genius. Your colleagues look at each other with raised eyebrows and shake their heads. When you return home, you look back on the incident and feel embarrassed. What the heck was that about? Where did that willingness to confront and make war over such a minor detail come from? You want to pick up the phone and call a buddy from work just to make sure everything is ok. Maybe you do actually call, and say, "That was so not like me!"

You may feel puzzled but I'm here to tell you this can happen to anyone at any given moment with the energy of Aries raining down. It's happened to me and it can happen to you. The only defense against this bizarre behavior is to recognize when you are being hit with this energy and then, and only then, can you take the steps to smooth it out and get through the day without declaring war on someone or something. Oh, Aries is a beautiful and passionate sign when *we* are in the driver's seat, but it's not such a pretty picture when these strong energies are leading the way and driving us.

Stirling Formula for the Time of Aries:

It is wonderful to have a pioneering spirit and to charge ahead with new beginnings but, in this month, be gentle with your friends and foes alike. Use your power to share kindness and understanding. Really think about this on a daily basis. Use your passion in a positive way.

Be very careful of your true motives this month. Research first and do not just jump into new endeavors. In other words, keep a lid on that compulsive behavior. By staying away from ego-based reactions, you can really use your higher senses. As Gandhi said, "Be the change you want to see in the world." Yes, that means you! You are powerful. If you start something, be sure to go the extra mile and finish it.

In this month, tasks may seem easy but, as you will se, completing tasks is easier said than done. Listen to the language of this energy. Completing a project or job, or even getting places on time, can mean a great deal. It will empower and please you to be complete with a job well done.

Your Daily Moon Energies:
Moon in Aries:

This may bring on a feeling of excitement and enthusiasm. You may feel ambitious and strong, eager to start projects, make changes, and share your vision with passion. Watch for impulsive action, head-on conflicts and selfishness. Balance this energy with good judgment. Be mindful of the rights of others. This is a good time for random acts of kindness.

The Time of Taurus
20 April – 20 May
Second Sign of the Zodiac
Element: Earth
Ruling Planet: Venus

ENERGIES OF TAURUS:

"Awaken now the energies of love and loyalty."

Taurus, the second sign of the zodiac, is symbolized by the constellation of the Bull. The positioning of this sign comes into alignment around the 20th of April each year, and is ruled by the planet Venus. The month of Taurus is IYAR in Hebrew.

The Bull carries the aspects of persistence, practicality, and loyalty. Taureans may also be stubborn and unyielding. Under Venus, they are known for their sensuality and earthiness. The energies of practicality, combined with great patience, are very powerful, especially when you add the energies of Venus. That is why those born under this sign may draw the opposite sex like bees to honey. However stubborn and pragmatic they may be, Taureans also possess a great deal of charm.

Venus brings in the energies and intelligence of the heart. Taureans are lovers of the arts. They recognize the beauty in life and are sensitive to self and others. The element of Earth brings with it wisdom of the ages and intelligence about matters of the body. Taureans are conscious that we are from the earth and to her we will return.

In the Way of Kabbalah:

The 30-day time frame of Taurus is unique to any other grouping. In this time more than any other, we may receive more light, more fulfillment from the Creator. In the way of Kabbalah, this month is called *IYAR*, which translates as 'to glow' because it is the 'Month of Light.'

In this month, the letter *BET* also connects us to the blessings. Are you living the light? Do you love this day beyond the personal, beyond your own story? This month is about communicating with the life force of the Creator that is infinite and present in each of us every moment. It is not about the *what* of life; it is about the *how* of life. See beyond the chaos; see the blessings, not the doubts.

Put your focus on who you are and invest energy in your dream. It will come. Be in the moment, right here, right now.

When we are ready, the blessings will be right here, right now. This month we can turn on the light, heal our emotions, and heal our lives. If you walk into a dark room and you don't like it, *turn on the light!* Replace misery with excitement. The switch is in your mind. Turn it on! Work through the challenges and the illusions ... and receive the light.

Life Example of Taurean Energy:

Each year I travel to Kauai in the Hawaiian Islands. It is one of the strongest energy vortexes on the planet and also one of the wettest places on the planet. One day I was with a friend and we decided to go to the southern end of the island to seek out a new beach area we had heard about. It can be sunny on the south end of Kauai while it is raining on the north end of the island. We drove to the southern tip and reached the coastline, but could not seem to find the beach we were looking for, despite driving around for hours. I know it sounds ridiculous to be on a small island and not be able to find the beach, but that is precisely what was happening to us. By late afternoon, my friend said, "Oh let's forget it and go back."

I said, "Hold on a moment. Let me see what position the moon is in today." I pulled out my pocket moon chart and sure enough, the moon was in Taurus. Knowing that saved the day! I knew that a Taurus moon meant many obstacles for the day, but also that because the sign is ruled by Venus, I had to feel with my heart. So we pulled over and said a small prayer to help us find our way to this missing beach. We had encountered many obstacles and now were determined to keep our eye on the goal. Persistence is the way to make it through a Taurus day.

So on we went with renewed hope. We meandered down some small streets and then, just like magic, we came to a parking lot that was next to a hotel. We realized the beach was hidden by this hotel, and so we parked and walked towards the sound of the ocean. Soon, we felt that warm and wonderful sand beneath our feet. The fact that we knew the influences of the day and the formula for that day helped us to work with the energies and, in the end, our goal was realized.

(It is important to note that although the format for this writing is in monthly cycles, every month—every moment of every month—affects each and every one of us. Please know that this is true no matter what sign we were born under.)

Stirling Formula for the Time of Taurus:

We know this is the sign of persistence and the power of perseverance. So, in this month, see the blessings, not the doubts. See the light at the end of the tunnel and get there no matter what it takes. Restrict any urge to give up; it is only an illusion that casts doubt on your goal.

In this month, you must be steadfast. Do not get sidetracked by the illusion. Every opportunity that comes into your life will be surrounded by illusion and trials. The planet Venus brings the energy of the heart. Your heart can decipher what is real and what is illusion. Look into your heart, see your goal and be persistent. Believe in yourself and know that success will be yours. You may at times be as stubborn as a bull, so restrict this, step back and take a deep breath. Look at all sides and follow your heart. Follow your true self and not your ego.

Your Daily Moon Energies: Moon in Taurus:

As the Moon enters Taurus, the aggressive and fiery energy of Aries becomes a bit more mellow and solid. You tend to move more slowly, preferring caution to impulse. At times, the energy of Taurus brings up obstacles, giving us an opportunity to keep our eye on the goal and lead with our hearts. Watch for stubbornness and holding on to the status quo. The need for financial and material security is strong during this time. This is a good time to appreciate and enjoy Mother Nature and practice random acts of kindness.

The Time of Gemini
21 May — 21 June
Third Sign of the Zodiac
Element: Air
Ruling Planet: Mercury

ENERGIES OF GEMINI:

"The channels of communication are open."

The constellation of the Twins begins on May 21ˢᵗ each year. The main characteristic of the sign of Gemini is communication. Quick in wit and enthusiastic in life, Gemini is sometimes referred to as 'the Eternal Child.' The month of Gemini is SIVAN in Hebrew.

Always seeking higher knowledge, Gemini is also the eternal student. Gemini's love conversation and mental stimulation. They usually have a sensitive nervous system. This can bring about restlessness and a feeling that there must be more. The planet Mercury brings out our expressiveness and, at times, a Gemini can seem most animated. Mercury brings with it the aspects of communication, deep thought and efficiency. The element of air brings in mental abilities and a feeling for spirit and thought.

In the Way of Kabbalah:

Gemini represents the third column, situated between the columns of Aries and Taurus. This center column gives us the ability to connect to the Creator on a seed level. The two aspects of giving and receiving become one. We can fix the frame of our consciousness and so affect our lives on a moment-to-moment basis. "Be concerned with the content, not the container." Energy for health and love are available, yet concealed.

Life Example of Gemini Energy:

It was early on a Saturday morning when the phone rang. A woman named Carol asked me to speak at a conference on the subjects of women's health, wellness and spirituality. I was happy to accept as I wrote down the information and carefully put the paper where I knew I would not misplace it. I prepared a talk I felt would be very exciting and useful. The week passed and my talk was about another week away. The phone rang; it was Carol, making sure I would be at the conference the next day. Oh my God! How could I have thought that the event was still a week away? It turns out that we'd had a miscommunication. What Carol had said and what I'd heard were two different things. In the time of Gemini energy, it is so very important to be very clear when you communicate. Double-check everything. Although the strong suite of Gemini is communication, it is also the downside, as *mis*communication can come into play. I was so grateful Carol had called me, otherwise I would have missed it altogether. So on the days that the moon is in Gemini, be very careful about communication and be sure everyone is on the same page and hearing the same things.

Stirling Formula for the Time of Gemini:

As we look at the formula for working with the energies of Gemini, we will see that communication is key in this month, as challenges in the form of misunderstanding could easily come into play. Look at both sides. Gemini is all about communication and now would be a great time to put those skills to work.

Investigate and learn about a given situation that may arise. Look inside the situation, as it may be different than it looks on the outside. For those of you ready to take the next step in your life, know that there is a time to study and a time to share. Perhaps the student is now ready to become the teacher.

Remain calm and restrain a quick reaction. You may see the truth unfold if you allow it some time. Balance your analysis, and beware of wanting to delve to deep into a situation. Guard against being nit-picky or scattered. Be extra gentle with your health and your love this month. The smallest act of kindness can go along way and may reveal new possibilities. Know with certainty that your connection is strong in this month. Be the light.

Your Daily Moon Energies:
Moon in Gemini:

This energy brings to us communication skills and the ability to see both sides of a situation. While the moon is in Gemini, we may feel so adaptable that we have a hard time making decisions. Activities that involve ideas, problem-solving and writing bode well. As mental energy is the focus of a Gemini Moon, watch for restlessness, words that may be overly spontaneous and hastily expressed. There may also be a rationalization of feelings.

The Time of Cancer
21 June – 22 July
Fourth Sign of the Zodiac
Element: Water
Ruling Planet: Moon

ENERGIES OF CANCER:

"Bring us the depth of caring and emotion as deep as the ocean."

Beginning on June 21st, Cancer, the constellation of the Crab, moves across our night sky and the moon shines its mystic and deep energies, many of us will be influenced by this awesome combination. The month of Cancer is pronounced TAMMUZ in Hebrew.

Cancer brings with it nurturing and the energies of motherhood. It also brings deep emotion and feeling, and the sign of Cancer may also bring with it feelings of depression or despair. Cancerians may have the desire to protect and hold on, not only to things, but to people as well.

In this month, we may feel extra sensitive and may become easily hurt if things do not go as we had planned. The Moon brings in the energies of deep emotion and mystery. This is the only sign that has 100 percent of the moon's attention. (It is a double whammy) This combination can be very challenging. Remember that cosmic energy is not our own, but just a reflection. Just as the moon reflects the light of the sun, so we reflect the light of the Cosmos. What's going on inside? What are you reflecting? This may be a time of internal and emotional cleansing.

The first day of the season of summer, June 21, is marked by the first day of the sign of Cancer. This cosmic event, the longest day of the year in the Northern Hemisphere, is also called "Ostara" by some as, from this point forward, the days will be getting shorter by about a minute a day, as we make our way towards the Autumn Equinox in the sign of Libra.

IN THE WAY OF KABBALAH:

The Kabbalah sees the sign of Cancer as a sign that will push buttons in a very specific way. It is a month when we have the opportunity to bring our cells and ourselves out of chaos and into divine order. Cancer is a disease of confused cells. This month, we can remove the confusion. Do not do things that will destroy your life. Do not connect yourself with confused energy, but rather walk in the energy of the light. This is not an easy month. We have the choice to get out of our comfort zone and cleanse that which is no longer in our highest good. In this month especially, promote consciousness of appreciation.

Life Example of Cancer Energy:

One day as I was driving to the grocery store, I began to feel very depressed and hopeless. It came on me suddenly, and I just felt awful. This is not who I am.

In fact, it was so opposite of who I am, I couldn't figure out what was going on. I thought maybe I was feeling the woes of the world or maybe this was a premonition. I moped around the store, and as I reached to open my car door, I began to cry. I felt as if the world was on my shoulders and I had nowhere to go and no one to turn to. I felt alone and confused. And then I thought: *What's going on? This is not like me. I must be grateful for every moment. Is it possible that I'm being hit with some cosmic energy?*

I sometimes forget I'm susceptible to these incoming energies, so I hurried home, put the groceries on the kitchen counter and ran into my office to see if this could be so. I pulled out my daily moon chart and what do you know! The moon was in Cancer that day and I had my answer to what was happening to my usual joyous mood. As soon as I knew that this could be the effect of cosmic forces, the fog began to lift and I simply said, "I am handing back this energy, for it is a reaction to the outside forces and I know I have a choice. I choose life and laughter." I began thinking of everything I have to be grateful for, and I said repeatedly, "I intend to feel good and happy."

Knowing that this energy would soon be gone really helped me to hang on. And knowing that once again this was not my authentic self but a reaction immediately brought me to a new level of understanding. I began calling my friends to check up on them and make sure they knew about the energy of the day. It turns out, I was not the only one wandering around like a lost soul that day. I know that having the knowledge of this cosmic event and the wisdom of how to deal with it helped every one I spoke with.

Stirling Formula for the Time of Cancer:

This is a month to gather your strength. Above all, *do not overreact*. Think about all that you have and all that you are. This is a month of great tests and inner reflection. Look around and think before you speak. Do not drown yourself in depression and self-questioning.

Know that these are the energies that are raining on us from the heavens. Take time this month to be grateful. Be sure and make some fun time for yourself. It is imperative that you take a deep breath this month, take a walk or have a picnic, and reflect on the positive. Know that transformation requires the falling away of *what was* to become *what will be*.

If feelings of jealously or possessiveness arise, take another deep breath and know that the only real control is to let go. If you feel over-emotional, it is great to have a good cry and move on, knowing that all is moving toward your highest good. Watch for the positive signs. See the light and the blessing in all things.

Day by day, we will get through these strong energies. On July 10, there is also the energy to heal and repair any disease in the body, not only physical but also mental and emotional. On this day, take some time to connect to Source. Meditate, put out good energy to all, and be thankful for all that is in your life. Breathe in the healing light and carry it with you. You may need it in this month of Cancer.

Your Daily Moon Energies: Moon in Cancer:

Remember, the Moon has no light of her own, only reflective light. So you may tend to go inward and be reflective of your life.

This is a time of heightened emotions and sensitivities. Reason takes a back seat, making this a vulnerable period. Be cautions of hurting others and allowing yourself to be wounded emotionally. In general, there may be moodiness and feelings of change on a moment-to-moment basis. The Cancer is caring, and the Moon brings out the motherly instinct. There is a tendency to overeat or over-indulge during this time. Practice kindness for yourself and others.

 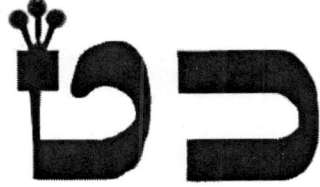

The Time of Leo
23 July – 23 August
Fifth sign of the Zodiac
Element: Fire
Ruling Planet: Sun

ENERGIES OF LEO:

"Ah Leo, the brightness and intensity of the sun shines within you."

On July 23rd, the constellation of the Lion starts its journey across our night sky. Called MENACHEM AV in the way of Kabbalah, Leo is perhaps the most powerful month of the year, bringing with it the aspects of vitality, power, nobility, generosity, and leadership. Leo is the only sign ruled by the Sun, therefore 100 percent of this energy is pouring down on our world in this short time span. The Sun brings in passion and the vitality of life force, which can bring about physical and spiritual healing energy. Be aware that this is extreme energy.

When the Sun rains down all of its power, it is a dynamic combination that can have global influences, not only on the side of light, but on the shadow side as well. The element of fire adds passion to all you think and do this month, making it a time of transformation.

In the Way of Kabbalah:

The Moon controls the way energy affects life. The Moon is a reflection of the Sun. The cosmic influences of this month are very strong. The Sun is the source of all healing because it is the physical manifestation of the light of the Creator. The Sun gives us Vitamin D. This month, we can connect directly to the totality of the life force of the Creator (the Source). In this month, we can heal in a powerful way ... or we can destroy in a powerful way. The most extreme disasters can happen in this month.

Ego correlates with Leo—power misused. When you pray for yourself only, it is the power of destruction. If you selfishly pray for money and it comes, it will be taken away somehow. If you receive wealth to do good with, to share, then miracles will happen. Does your desire to receive include others? Is your power used to help others? To work together for one humanity? Do you have the consciousness of love to care for others?

Cosmically, all the energy everywhere becomes more intense this month. More energy, more light is present, and for some, more power, more ego, more shadow. This month, spiritual work is the hardest. This month, we have all the energy. The question is, how do we choose to use it?

Life Example of Leo Energy:

This is a perfect example of how we can be blind-sided by an energy. In August 2005, I went to visit a dear friend. She had moved into town not to long before and felt uncertain about driving, so she asked if I would drive her to the store to do some shopping. The 'ego of Leo' was beaming down as I gave her my long list of excuses for the day. "I have a full day! I'm expected at an art gallery opening and then I need to show my handmade jewelry to some one and then, so perhaps another day when I have more time." I got up from my chair with the utmost of confidence and headed for the door. As I reached for the door, I had a big flash of realization! *Hold on. Stop for a moment and breath. What's happening to me? This is not like me at all and certainly not a reflection of who I am.*

I stopped, turned, and started laughing out loud. "Wow!" I said. "I just got hit with some Leo energy! What was that about?" I looked at my friend, apologized for the ego attack and said, "I'd love to take you to the store. Your friendship is a precious jewel to me."

While driving in the car, she asked me what happened. I explained, "Sometimes we can get hit with a strong energy surge of the ruling planet in that day. I realized that I was being a puppet to the energy of Leo and that I had a choice, because I know about this energy. Once you identify it, you can feel the difference between when you're acting in your authentic self versus reacting to the energies at hand. It's a useful and valuable tool."

Back at her home, we talked for an hour and I went on my way feeling fulfilled and happy that I was able to help my friend. I left, still chuckling about how close I'd come to being less than my authentic self. It can happen to any of us at any time.

(Please note that if the daily moon chart shows that the moon is in Leo for that day, you are subject to the same energy, even if the Sun is in any sign other than Leo.)

Stirling Formula for the Time of Leo:

WOW! Where to start? In this month, we must above all check our egos at the door. This is the time to be thankful every day and keep in your mind sharing and healing for the good of the all. Immerse yourself in the positive energies of the Sun. Channel creativity, vitality and the willpower to steer clear of ego and pride.

The shadow side will be very strong in this month, so just get through it day by day. Stand in the light, be patient and kind, and practice compassion. This may not be as easy as it sounds. Restrict a quick reaction and the emotion of anger. Find the blessing; it is there I promise you.

Step back from those in your life who would make war with you. Show compassion to others and be gentle with yourself. Stand firm on your boundaries and keep an eye out for those who would misuse you in any way. Be aware of the shadow powers of this month. Keep yourself planted firmly in the light, and you will come through this time stronger and many vibrations higher.

Your Daily Moon Energies:
Moon in Leo:

The Sun is ruler of Leo, the great healer. This is a time of romance, affection, attention and recognition. There is optimism in the air. Limitations are ignored and new heights of leadership can be achieved. Be cautious of runaway ego, and dominant behavior. You may feel as if you're right and will make war over any opposition. Restrict this impulse. This is a perfect time to practice random acts of kindness and generosity.

The Time of Virgo
23 August – 22 September
Sixth Sign of the Zodiac
Element: Earth
Ruling Planet: Mercury

ENERGIES OF VIRGO:

"We welcome your neatness and organization."

On August 23rd, with the energies of Virgo coming in, we may feel compelled to delve into every detail of every situation. Although it is a good idea to know fully a situation, beware of nit-picking and overdoing it. The month of Virgo is pronounced ELUL in the way of Kabbalah.

Virgo brings in the energies of efficiency, discernment and the analytical ethic. Virgos like order and can be quite perfectionist. The energies of Virgo are very sensitive, and Virgos do not like having their faults pointed out. Because the time of Virgo is so sensitive, those born under this sign can be susceptible to tension and anxiety, and be extra sensitive. And so, as this energy rains down, we may all be more susceptible to feelings of tension and anxiety in this month.

Virgos do not like clutter; they like to see everything neat and in it place. The element of earth brings in a practical energy as well as a nurturing and creative one. The planet Mercury rains down the positive energies of cleverness and mental agility, good communication skills and intellect. But let us not forget that Mercury also brings in the shadow energies of trickiness and lack of logic.

In the Way of the Kabbalah:

This is a time of Spiritual Transformation. The time of *Rosh Hashanah*. As the rabbi would say, "This event is not one born of man, but is a cosmic event." This is a time when the destiny of every creation, every being, has the opportunity to open up to a new reality. This is an opportunity to put down the pain and the fear, and create a new spiritual transformation, an opportunity to clear the need for judgment.

The time of Virgo is a time to look within, reflect and heal ourselves. Yes, it is a time to heal, a time to connect with the light for the higher good of ourselves and all. In this next 22 days, the Cosmos is helping us to prepare for the next month, when we may set the course for the next year.

There is a Kabbalist ritual I find very symbolic called 'Empty Your Pockets.' According to the ancient ways, at this time of year filled with daily thoughts and deliberation, you would be filling your pockets with judgments, with the pain of yesterdays and the fear of tomorrows. After many days of this, you would put a piece of bread in your pocket.

You would find your way to a body of water, a lake, a stream, a river, an ocean. Putting your hands in your pockets, you would hold on to the piece of bread and charge it with all the negative energy of the yesterdays, the judgments, the pain and the fears. You would charge the bread and then empty your pockets into the water, letting all the negative thoughts be washed away.

Do this. Wash away all that belongs to the: "I used to be …," and to judgment. The reality is to search your soul and acknowledge any self-doubts or negativity. Then empty yourself of these self-defeating energies. Symbolically allow them to wash away, opening yourself to new growth and sharing.

When we judge someone or something, it is a judgment of the self. When we judge without mercy and compassion, we judge ourselves. This is an opportunity to put yourself in another's shoes and feel what that person might feel. When the need for judgment falls away, that is a defining moment in your conscious evolution.

The moment you change the way you feel about a situation, that is the Transforming Moment. At that moment, everything negative will fade away, and you will have enlightened yourself to a greater place of understanding and light. The washing away of all that belongs to the "I used to be ..." is what *Rosh Hashanah* and this month of Virgo is all about.

LIFE EXAMPLE OF VIRGO ENERGY:

I know you are expecting a story of someone so neat it drives you crazy. Or someone who nit-picks you to death. These could all be come under the description of Virgo energy. But this is a story of a brilliant engineer who was such a sensitive soul, he had a very rough time dealing with life. He was sensitive but his inner voice was very critical of others. Secretly he would make life a bit easier for himself by judging others, not realizing he was only judging himself. He was very educated and felt superior to everyone—this can also be a Virgo trait. He seemed to be well-liked and well-respected. If he could only keep his inner voice quiet. We became friends, maybe because I accepted his quiet arrogance. I spent much time in discussion with him about how he has a choice in every moment to start a new. He would tell me how unhappy he was, and yet my words seemed to have no effect, as he chose to go on the way he was. He received a payoff from this by eliciting sympathy from those who saw how unhappy he was. So I guess you could say sometimes when you feel critical of and superior to others, perhaps it is a day when the moon is in Virgo. On those days when the world around you looks like it needs fixing, that's the time to do the work on *yourself*. As you shed how you used to be and heal your inner self, all of a sudden, the whole world around you begins to change for the better. The time is now to really make an effort to understand and be compassionate of others, and to remember we're all in this together.

Stirling Formula for the Time of Virgo:

As this constellation moves into view, we may feel a desire to criticize others. Restrict this urge. Know that this is the energy at work, and that you need not fall prey to it. Use your skills of communication to really listen and consider the other view. Remember that everyone is seeking to become his or her higher self. Journaling this month may be very healing. Replace the urge to judge with patience and kindness. This may take effort due to the influence of Mercury.

If you find yourself wanting to play a trick on someone, or if you find others illogical and feel superior to them, get over it! Know it is the ego and the trickster in Mercury. Take some time to relax and unwind. Just do it! Take a whole day, or even an hour or two, and keep connected to how your heart really feels. Come from that place.

Take the time to listen to your heart and honor the energy of your inner self. This month will breeze by. Look toward making a new friend.

Your Daily Moon Energies:
Moon in Virgo:

Virgo likes intellectual pursuits, especially those that require attention to detail. People are usually shy and withdrawn during this phase. They tend to be more discriminating and can become easily critical. Cleanliness and health are at the forefront of today's energy.

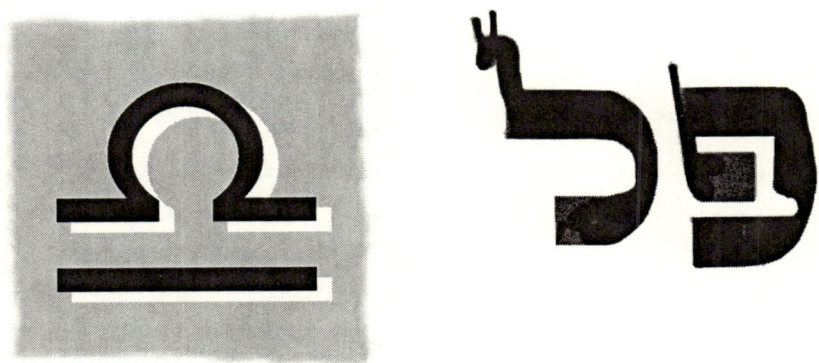

The Time of Libra
23 September – 22 October
Seventh sign of the Zodiac
Element: Air
Ruling Planet: Venus

ENERGIES OF LIBRA:

"How beautiful and artistic are the energies of Libra."

Beginning on September 23rd, the Sun is in the sign of Libra, the constellation of the Balancing of Two Weights. Libra is also the month of TISHREI in the way of Kabbalah. We see this symbol for justice everywhere in our society, outside of courthouses and in front of government buildings. Some of the aspects of this sign are balance, both in thought and behavior, diplomacy, harmony and intellectual ability. Libras are friendly; they like to be popular and are outgoing socially. They seek justice in all things. In fact, sometimes they are so good at seeing both sides, they become indecisive and find it difficult to come to a conclusion.

The element of air aids in communication and vision. The planet Venus brings in the beauty of the heart, the desire to help. Many people born under this sign become artists and view life through the eyes of one seeking beauty in all things. But Venus is more than the planet of love and beauty; it also represents the divine feminine, the heart of the goddess. Relating to what brings pleasure and the expression of love itself, Venus is warmth and has a softening effect on the energies of this month.

The Autumn Equinox is marked by the first day of the sign of Libra, September 21. The Equinox signifies the great balance, the beginning of Autumn, the first day of the fall season. The last of the harvest has been reaped and is stored for the coming winter months. This begins the long period of the coming darkness of winter, and all of nature makes ready for the Winter Solstice in the sign of Capricorn.

In the Way of Kabbalah:

This month sees the high holiday of *Rosh Hashana*. It connects us to the power of the Creator. In this time we can fully connect to the light of Source. Libra is loving and easy-going, bringing harmony to the universe. Seeing beauty in all things. Sometimes the easy going Libra finds it a challenge to take action. Time to bring harmony into our own world. You give, so give to yourself as well.

Life Example of Libran Energy:

My dear mother (may she rest in peace) was a wonderful artist. She saw the beauty in all things, especially in nature. She loved to paint flowers, mountains and trees, and had a way of capturing the essence of whatever she was painting. It was as if she could feel the soul of the flower and translate that feeing to canvas. It was amazing to see.

She was also born under the sign of Libra. You would think that this would mean that her life was always in balance. The truth is that many times, it is *striving* for balance that is the life lesson for Libra. Often the energy of Libra will have you doing things for others that sometimes may tread on your boundaries. A moment of indecision or confusion can lead to someone feeling used or feeling out of balance. I remember my mother would be very matter-of-fact about something and then really make an effort to see the other side. She had a keen sense of things and was the gentle soul of our family. The lesson here is that when the moon crosses Libra, we sometimes get a little confused about our boundaries. In an effort to keep the peace, you may find yourself compromising more than you had intended. So watch for this and hold strong to your own sense of balance; trust your intuition. Listen to your inner voice. Remember you are the beauty and you are the divine expression. Believe in yourself, for all the wisdom of the universe resides deep within you.

Stirling Formula for the Time of Libra:

The key word for this month is *balance*. Find your place of balance. This month, seek justice in all that you do, and in all things. I know you will want everything to be in harmony, but be careful, and don't let others tread on your boundaries. This month, you may find some tests in this area.

Your loving nature needs a dose of reality now and then. Look at all sides and let your heart decide that which is real. It is difficult to imagine shadow energies when it comes to Venus but alas, it is true. Beware of idleness, overindulgence and ego-based pleasure. The way is open to divine energy. Let your higher self lead the way through the energies of this month ... and all will bloom before your eyes.

Your Daily Moon Energies:
Moon in Libra:

During this period, you may feel a sensitivity and an attraction for others. This is a good time for projects requiring teamwork. And a good time for friendships and marriage. A friendly and tolerant vibe is evident. You can feel drawn to harmony and balance. This a good time for social gatherings and artistic endeavors. This sign brings in the energy of "balance" and, as always, a great time to practice random acts of kindness.

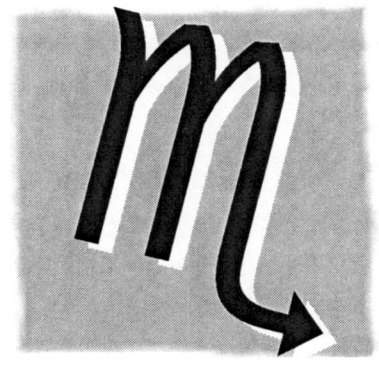 

The Time of Scorpio
23 October – 22 November
Eighth Sign of the Zodiac
Element: Water
Ruling Planet: Pluto/Mars

ENERGIES OF SCORPIO:

"Dedication and passion reign."

In Hebrew, the month of Scorpio is called Mar CHESHVAN, and its bold energy begins October 23rd each year. As the seasons change and the constellation of the Scorpion moves into our night sky, it rains down the energies of strength and dominance. This time carries with it the seed for a dynamic personality, someone sensual and mystical who draws the attention of all who come near. It is difficult to escape the hypnotic gaze of the Scorpio. Because Scorpios feel deeply and can be easily hurt, they usually like to be in control and can be very secretive and revengeful. The sting of the Scorpion will not soon be forgotten.

This is a water sign and so carries deep emotion. Paradoxically, some Scorpios can be cold and lacking in emotion. The planet Pluto rules Scorpio, and is named for the god of the underworld who reigns over transformation, death and rebirth. This planet signifies deep change, and brings in both positive and shadow aspects. On the positive side, Pluto brings to the table regenerative capabilities, the possibility for transformation and revealing what is hidden. On the shadow side of Pluto lie obsession and compulsion, and the potential for abuse of power. Mars brings in a feeling of impulsiveness and competitiveness. Mars also brings in the courageous heart and a willingness to be very enterprising and sometimes temperamental.

In the Way of Kabbalah:

The sign of Scorpio is looked upon as a sign of extremes. Love or hate. Friend or foe. It is an overly-emotional sign with a heavy sting. All water signs are emotional. However in the way of Kaballah it is thought that the sign of Scorpio in irrational in there emotion. Being polarized, black and white, no middle ground. Power and control, determination and strength. Scorpio is a fixed sign which means they do not like change. Great in business and in politics. It is always best to stay on the good side of a Scorpio.

Life Example of Scorpio Energy:

This is not so much a story but a situation. I have a dear friend, Annie, who shares some of her challenges with me. I would like to share some with you and perhaps you will see some similarities in your own feelings. One day, Annie told me, "I cannot stand to let my boyfriend out of my sight. I feel like the only time he has fun is when he's away from me. I'm happiest when I'm in total control and know every second of his day. I just feel that if I don't have control, he'll leave me."

I replied, "You know, the only way we're really in control is to let go of all control. The only thing you need to control is your desire to have control. No one wants to be ruled by anyone else, so lighten up and connect yourself with the good and not the doubt. Listen to logic and not run away from fear."

There are times when we can get hit with a beam of jealousy or fear, or a sudden impulse to be in control. This is sometimes what Scorpion energy can feel like. My friend Annie is a Scorpio and on the days when the moon is in Scorpio, she feels a double whammy of this intense energy. This is what evolvement is all about. Breathe and know how you do not like to be controlled. Then extend that freedom and understanding to those around you. Scorpio is deep and beautiful, so relax and know that love is not possession. Connect with the good and share your light.

Stirling Formula for Scorpio:

In this month, beware of the all-or-nothing attitude. Not everything in life is a competition. Not everything is black and white. Resist the quick reaction and vengeful feelings. Look into your heart and come from a place of compassion. Know that if feelings of jealously or possessiveness arise, these are due to outside forces.

Take a deep breath. You can make the choice to stand on the side of positive transformation. Curtail secretive activities and be honest with yourself and others. Welcome change; perhaps there is something wonderful on the horizon. The key word for this month is moderation. Beware of extremes and over-emotion this month.

Remember that sometimes, things are not in our control and the only true control is to let go. Yes, I said, "Let go."

Your Daily Moon Energies: Moon in Scorpio:

When the Moon is in Scorpio, there is an increase in emotional intensity and people take offense easily. Strong passions and desires are the order of business. Stay away from social situations that are potentially complicated, and beware of jealousy. Be careful when interacting with the opposite sex. However, it is an excellent time for deep merging on an emotional level. A Scorpio Moon is a good time for surgical procedures except for areas of the Scorpio zone, which are the bladder, uterus, sexual organs. However, it is an excellent time for any necessary research and investigation. And an excellent time for random acts of kindness.

 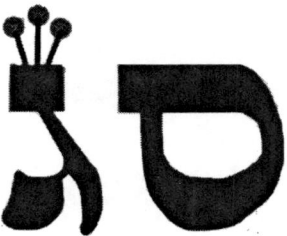

The Time of Sagittarius
22 November – 21 December
Ninth Sign of the Zodiac
Element: Fire
Ruling Planet: Jupiter

ENERGIES OF SAGITTARIUS:

"Ah, Sagittarius, your aim is keen."

The constellation of the Archer begins on November 22nd each year, and the month of Sagittarius is called KISLEV in Hebrew. Sagittarians are free spirits with a friendly and independent attitude. The energies of this sign compel us to feel intuitive and idealistic, very honest and clever, and genuinely seeking good for all.

You may feel adventurous at this time, looking at the "big plan" and desiring to improve on what is. The archer aims far into the distance, and the element of fire fuels the powerful emotions of this sign. In ancient times referred to as 'the lord of truth,' the planet Jupiter brings in the energies of mental, emotional and spiritual expansion. You may feel a yearning to travel to far away, exotic places this month, as Jupiter likes change through travel. The positive, beneficent energies of Jupiter promote truth and optimism, while the shadow energies push us toward exaggeration, false optimism, even greed. Over-confidence is also on this menu.

In the Way of Kabbalah:

Oh Sagittarius, you do love a good challenge. Some may even say you are a daredevil. You see the whole picture but what about the details? Have you kept your promises? You love change and thrive on excitement. Focus on sharing in an honest way and you will find yourself standing in the light. This is the time of the miracle of lights that is called *Hanukah*. As we light each candle, so we shut out the darkness.

Life Example of Sagittarian Energy:

As I opened my eyes on that Thursday morning, it felt like a computer switched on. There were all of a sudden long list of "must do today" running through my head and I hadn't even brushed my teeth yet. I had a quick bite and off I went out to conquer the world. Boy I felt great! As I was getting in my car

I saw the mountains in the distance. All of a sudden I felt spellbound, captured for a moment and everything left my head except the feeling that I must go to the mountains. I sat in my car for a moment, now thoroughly confused and as I looked over into the passenger seat there was my daily moon guide. I decided to see what was up? I saw that the moon was in Sagittarius that day. It gave me comfort to know that I was not really wigging out but was just being hit with the overwhelming rushing energy of Sagittarius combined with the feeling that I want to escape to some distant adventure. I knew to slow down and do one thing at a time today. I knew that my kindness and sincerety would be so welcomed and appreciated as well. It was calming just to have the information and I couldn't help but smile throughout the day as I watched people franticly running around as they were being pushed by the the rushing energy of Sagittarius.

Stirling Formula for the Time of Sagittarius:

In this month, pay attention to what is happening around you. The urge to say whatever is on your mind will be strong. Think before you speak. It may seem easier to follow rather than to lead, but be sure you have good boundaries and can discern between helping others and enabling them.

Be careful about being extravagant this month, as it can turn to self-indulgence and greed. Be aware, keep your ego in its place and watch for any signs of its inflation. Check to be sure you are coming from the heart. Stay in the now. Be more sensitive to others. Let your truthful and friendly nature lead your way this month. Continue reaching for inner wisdom and you will sail through just fine.

Your Daily Moon Energies: Moon in Sagittarius:

Do you feel in a rush? The moon in Sagittarius pushes us to do more, be more. We feel more idealistic during this phase of the Moon, and restlessness is the order of the day. A desire of adventure and the outdoors persists. People are generally warm and friendly during this period, however there is also a strong need for independence. This sign puts a philosophical influence in the air and a desire for self-improvement, so it's a good time for a seminar and dealing with intuitions of learning. Practice kindness for yourself and others.

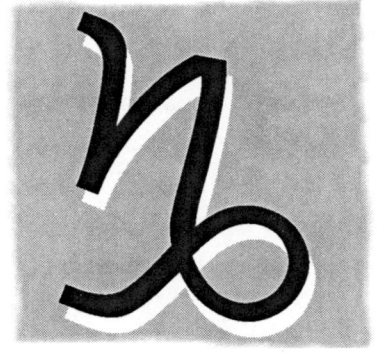 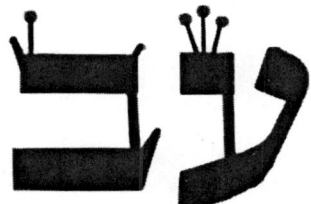

The Time of Capricorn
22 December — 20 January
Tenth Sign of the Zodiac
Element: Earth
Ruling Planet: Saturn

ENERGIES OF CAPRICORN:

"Hard-working, diligent, and driven, that's the 'Goat."

The constellation of Capricorn the Goat comes into view on December 22, bringing with it the energies of ambition and organization coupled with a strong sense of duty. The

Hebrew letters for Capricorn are Vav Vav Lamed and the month of Capricorn is called TEVET.

Hard-working and diligent, people born under this sign are compelled to have a purpose or they may feel lost. Structure can help a Capricorn feel complete. The element of earth brings in practical energies and a desire for prestige.

On the positive side, Capricorns love higher learning, common sense and the truth. This sign's shadow side is a leaning toward the controversial; one may fall into dishonesty. Saturn brings in the energies of wisdom, along with discipline and order. And beware of the shadow energies of fear and overreaction.

December 22, the first day of Capricorn, also marks the winter solstice, when the sun is the farthest south. In the Northern Hemisphere, we know this as "the shortest day of the year," the time to enter hibernation, the time of inner transformation. Winter is upon us, but it won't be long before the turning of the wheel, as we look towards the birth of the next spring.

In the Way of Kabbalah:

In this month, we are being given the opportunity to: "Think outside the box." This is the wisdom and message of Capricorn. To grasp this concept, we must first understand that thinking *inside* the box means that we believe a situation, whatever it may be, is 100 percent real. When you think inside the box, you may have thoughts such as, "I've been dealt a hard life, so I guess I'll just have to grin and bear it," or "He can never change," or "I guess I'll never be happy or rich or ..."

Thinking inside the box means that what you see cannot be changed; it means that the only solution to a problem is the one you can consciously think of. Restrict this reactive thought.

Thinking *outside* the box requires that you find a quiet place within yourself where you can see beyond the illusion. In this month of Capricorn, constantly remind yourself to open your awareness and learn to find new solutions to old problems. When we remind ourselves that all things are from the light and that all obstacles and challenges are merely opportunities to grow, we find the opportunity and become grateful in every moment. You will see your life changing in a positive way.

Life Example of Capricorn Energy:

Nancy, a friend of mine called me to complain about a situation with her boyfriend Bob, whom she has been seeing for about four months. "I feel like if I don't hurry up and fit in to what Bob wants me to be, he'll break up with me. He has this illusion about what our relationship should look like and if I don't comply, that will be it! How can anyone be so cut and dried? Why doesn't he see all the good aspects of us? He seems to be supportive of me and we have a great time together, but it's just this underlying feeling that none of his relationships work out so why should this one?"

As she was telling me this story, I related it to a similar story of my own. I wasn't surprised when she told me Bob was a Capricorn. I explained, "He hasn't come out of the box yet! He's in his own illusion of what the two of you should be like. It's almost like he came into the relationship just waiting for the other shoe to drop. This is the complexity of Capricorn."

I am afraid I did not have much advice for her except, "Encourage him that your relationship could flourish if he could relax a bit and not give in to these fixed illusions. And accept you for who you are and how you are."

This energy can hit us when the constellation of Capricorn filters through the Moon's energy. It's at this time we need to think of new ideas and new solution to old challenges.

Stirling Formula for the Time of Capricorn:

As we move through the lunar month of Capricorn (this applies to the daily moon in Capricorn as well), the main stumbling block you will face is fighting the illusion that the circumstances of your life are fixed. Saturn may try to throw in fear and doubt, but Saturn will also help you in this month to take a moment, search your heart and come from a place of wisdom and truth. Throw out your doubts and know with certainty that there are no real limitations, only the ones you put on yourself. Let go of limiting thinking. See beyond the illusion and restrict the ego.

You possess the true power to be your highest self. Be rigorously honest with yourself and others. Search your heart for truth. Restrict your desire to be controversial. Moderation is a good thing to remember when the energies of Capricorn are around us. And remember: "By putting the spiritual above the physical, everything is possible."

Your Daily Moon Energies:
Moon in Capricorn:

Work and duty are the energies of Capricorn. The drive is for status and financial security. You can become insensitive, so be aware of this. Don't ask for credit during this phase of the Moon. Apply yourself to the tasks of the day and stay in the present. Check for negativity and, as always, this is an excellent time for random acts of kindness.

The Time of Aquarius
20 January – 18 February
Eleventh Sign of the Zodiac
Element: Air
Ruling Planet: Saturn/Uranus

ENERGIES OF AQUARIUS:

"Oh Aquarius, alluring, sensitive and mysterious, your aloofness causes us to seek you out, to try and discover your mysteries."

Aquarius glides into our view beginning on January 20th each year, and it is the Hebrew month of SHEVET. The aspects and energies of this sign are very independent and unconventional, and may at times seem detached. This sign brings with it the energies of intuition. Aquarians like to be observers, cherishing their freedom. They like to do things their own way and do not want to be tied down. But Aquarians are also humanitarians who desire justice. They are very inventive and can sometimes get lost in the big picture. Those of this sign are friendly and helpful but can, at times, be very contrary. The element of air ushers in an opening to spirit.

Saturn brings in the energies of the wise, old man. In ancient mythology, this planet was known as "Old Father Time." Saturn symbolizes the laws of cause and effect, encouraging social order. Saturn also brings in the energy of structure and limitations.

Saturn beams down discipline and order, responsibility and wisdom, and the ability to see that which is real. Saturn also has a shadow influence that brings in the energy of fear and pessimism and over-restrictiveness. The influence of Uranus may bring in some distractions, disruptions and sudden changes in plans.

In the Way of Kabbalah:

Aquarius means to join together the physical and spiritual world. This month gives us the ability to bridge between the light and the vessel, between fulfillment and desire. We can eliminate darkness through the sharing of light. Start to see the manifestation of your work. See the big picture. The sign of Aquarius invites us to think outside the box. We can eliminate darkness from people's lives by sharing the light. The letter *BET* that makes up part of the sign of Aquarius means "to join together physical and spiritual worlds."

Life Example of Aquarian Energy:

It was a bright spring day and I was driving to a meeting when someone called on my cell phone and asked if I could stop and pick up something for them on the way. I said, "Oh sure, no problem," and headed to the store which was on my way to the meeting. As I parked my car, I got another call from someone else needing a favor. I thought: *This is strange. I'll be late to the meeting if I keep this up.*

I went into the store and got the item for the first friend. Just then, a third call came in and ... you guessed it, they needed a favor, so I said, "I'll get back to you."

As I drove down the beltway, I saw the beautiful Red Rocks Park and the mountains in the distance, and all I could think about was just forgetting about everything and going to the mountains. I wondered: *Am I not supposed to go to this meeting?* My car almost kept going towards the mountains on its own. I felt very confused, and just wanted to keep on driving forever. I pulled over and picked up the moon guide which was on my front seat. I discovered that the moon was in Aquarius, and realized that perhaps this accounted for the many different distractions. I just closed my eyes and took a few deep breaths and let my head rest for a moment and centered myself within my heart. Within a few minutes, I knew what to do. I got back on the road and delivered the item to my friend, and then went to the meeting which only lasted an hour, leaving plenty of time for me to go to the mountains for an hour or so. I knew people may be calling all day long to ask a favor, so I shut off my phone for a while to enjoy the bright spring day. In the energies of Aquarius, it is so important to be centered and not allow outside forces to confuse you. I also knew I may feel flighty and just say, "To heck with everything," and go off by myself. So I thought of a way to do all my errands and still get away as well. So with a little creativity and self-restraint, I made it through the day just fine. Oh and the other favor I did later that evening as it turned out to be a dinner invitation.

Stirling Formula for the Time of Aquarius:

This is a wonderful month to be friendly and helpful. Be aware that this is different than allowing yourself to be used. Bring in your communication skills and contemplate the wisdom within. In the month of Aquarius, one can sometimes become so involved with the big picture, the details can get lost. So in this month, pay attention to the details.

Share what you feel. Perhaps it will help all of humanity. Think outside the box. This means being creative and finding a way to your goal. A new challenge may not be solved by the old thinking. Take some time to think things out and come up with new solutions. There may be some new adventure on the horizon. So for this month, be prepared for the unexpected. Be aware of your need to be free and your sometimes flighty ways. Be aware that this may be an obstacle in itself if it goes unchecked. Remain centered and all will go as planned.

Your Daily Moon Energies:
Moon in Aquarius:

The strength of this moon cycle is to bridge the world above with the world below. This energy is friendly, but impersonal. During this time, there is an increased interest in the social welfare of others coupled with a desire for freedom. Innovative ideas are more likely to meet with interest and approval, as intellectual, rather than emotional, motivations are the driving force. Aquarius puts friends and friendships first and foremost. This is a good time for club or group meetings, and to practice warmth and kindness.

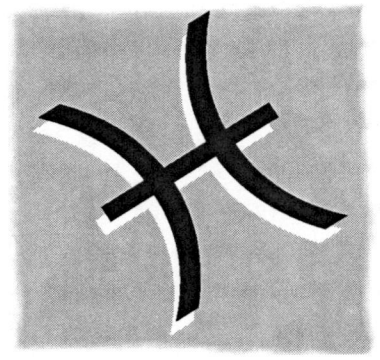 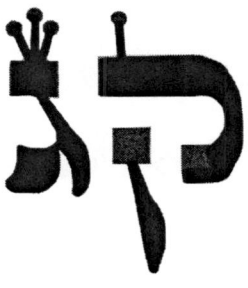

The Time of Pisces
19 February – 20 March
Twelfth Sign of the Zodiac
Element: Water
Ruling Planet: Neptune/Jupiter

ENERGIES OF PISCES:

"Piscean transcendence, sensitivity and wisdom complete the Big Wheel in the sky."

And so we come to the twelfth sign of the zodiac, Pisces, the constellation of Two Fish. Beginning on February 19th, the month of ADAR in the way of Kaballah carries with it wisdom from all the other signs in the zodiac. The aspect of transcendence is strong in this sign, yet the time of Pisces also spills over with sensitivity.

Pisceans are compassionate and kind, known for their psychic abilities and intense understanding. These water creatures can be visionaries and chameleons who fit in any environment. The ruling planet of Neptune brings in the aspects of dreaminess, illusion and seeing the world through rose-colored glasses, while enhancing the psychic abilities of the Piscean. Neptune is also known for its shadow side of delusion and addiction. The element of water gives this sign a triple whammy in the deep emotion category. So sensitive and creative, Pisceans often retreat into a world of magic and mystery. The influence of Jupiter causes the Piscean to think big and strive for higher wisdom. Jupiter also adds extra enthusiasm for the Pisces and they will champion a good cause.

In the Way of Kabbalah:

It is said that the last incarnation one makes into this world is to that of a fish. Pisces represents the restoration of the balance in nature, as this sign comes in the time of the Vernal Equinox, that great balance between dark and light. The true mystic, a Piscean's inner wisdom and direct connection to Source will keep this fish swimming in the enlightened direction.

Life Example of Piscean Energy:

This is a difficult one for me as I myself am a Pisces. I really like and understand the beautiful and aloof female of the species. The male Pisces, however, is a puzzle. I have noticed for me, a Pisces man can be very wishy-washy and tell you what you want to hear. (Scorpios sometimes engage in this behavior, as well, but they are not wishy-washy.) I was in Hawaii one year doing my spiritual work, and on my second day there, a Pisces man hugged me so tight, he broke two ribs. Then a few days later, I met a Pisces man who seemed to be interested in me ... only it became clear he was interested in what I might be able to do for his career, and nothing personal. So sometimes the gentle, mystic fish can be very charming when out for their own gain. I kept wondering: *Do I do this? Am I this way? Why is this being shown to me?*

When the energies of Pisces hit, we can be indecisive and flip-flop. One minute, we like the direction things are going ... and the next minute we don't. This is usually the time to get centered and call up your higher self. Practice rigorous honesty. Restrict the urge to manipulate. If addiction of any kind is an issue for you, be extra careful on the days the moon passes through Pisces.

Stirling Formula for the Time of Pisces:

Stand steady and do not hide away. Keep your heart and your visions in the light. Be direct in your thoughts and actions. Moderation is a key word in this month, so be careful not to overdo any kind of libation. Stay here with us this month and share your kindness and compassion. Be clear that kindness is not weakness, and keep an eye out for those who might try to take advantage of you.

You may want to fly away to your dream world, but know you are wanted and needed here on this plane. Stay connected to your higher self and, if you find yourself in a pity party or in delusion, restrict it. Know that these energies are very strong at this time. Look into your heart and allow your highest good to lead the way. Who said fish cannot fly?

Your Daily Moon Energies: Moon in Pisces:

The energies of intuition and imagination are strong during this time. You are generally gentle and kind, but easily discouraged. There can be deep spiritual insights and a drive toward self-sacrifice. A Pisces Moon is a good time for meditation and prayer. Take time for yourself. Kindness for all, always.

Epilogue

Go forth with the knowledge that you carry all within. As you explore and understand the language of the cosmos, you lift your vibrational signature and so become the co-creator in the world around you and within you. In allowing the transformation and allowing the intelligence of your heart to lead the way, you step into your true self—your true optimal self—and soothe the yearning in your spirit as your soul's purpose is revealed.

As the wheel turns, each season brings new information and the embracing of new technologies and human potential findings. So each year you may notice some of the languaging in this writing changing so as to keep on the farthest edge of these discoveries. For example, for a long time we have been referencing 'our higher self.' There is new languaging that validates there is truly no 'higher self' as we embrace knowledge and wisdom; instead, we step into our 'FULL POTENTIAL SELF,' or OPTIMAL SELF.

We live in an exciting time. Let us grow into and go forth as full potential beings, realizing that everything on and in this earth is so precious. We are the stewards of this beautiful planet and it is time to love and honor our mother earth and so ensure a sustainable future for our children and generations to come.

May the energies of the Cosmos shine upon you, illuminate you, and may you be held in the arms of the angels.

Bright blessings to you.

Sheila Z..Stirling

Glossary

Ancient Technologies: Refers to wisdom and technologies handed down from generation to generation. These are teachings that have stood the test of time and are relevant in the present time.

Astral: That which resembles the stars. A reference to the stars, space or skyward.

Boundaryless: The full experience of non-confined space and time.

Cosmos: The Universe, God, encompassing All That Is.

Ethereal: The ethereal body is made up of pure energy, highly refined and of a higher vibration. This energy body surrounds our physical form. The word "ethereal" comes from the Latin word "ether."

Evolution: This is usually a gradual change. With the passage of time, each generation is evolving and one can look back at the root and clearly see the difference. At this time, we are experiencing a quantum leap as we move from a three-dimensional world into the realms of the fourth dimension and beyond. For many of us, this is happening very quickly. It is the time of a great evolution for us all.

Global: This pertains to the entire Earth, the All of this planet.

Imperative: Urgent and important. A plea that time is of the essence. Do it now or suffer the consequences.

Kabbalah: Abraham the Great wrote down this ancient wisdom over 4,000 years ago. It is the technology that shares with us the code of creation. Its teachings include the facts that all is energy and energy is light. We as humans were meant to share this light in loving compassion for all.

Zodiac: The name given to the system of constellations that make up the 12 astrological signs.

Planets

Please note: the planets are in the order of their relationship to the sun and not in alphabetical order.

Sun: The Sun is a luminary and the source of all light and warmth on this planet. The planets in this "solar" system revolve around the sun and make up what we know on this planet as time. For example, it takes 365 days for the Earth to rotate around the Sun, thus making up one year of our time line. The Sun rules the sign of Leo.

Moon: The Moon has no light or warmth of its own, although it is also considered a luminary. It is also used as a marker of time on this planet. As the planets rotate around the sun, it is the moon that reflects the light of the sun in our night sky and so gives us the ever-present security that we are never in true darkness. There is one night each month that the sky is dark. It is the time of the "new moon" or "dark moon." This absence of reflective light marks the beginning of a new cycle that our planet embarks on, on its journey around the sun. The Moon rules the sign of Cancer.

Mercury: The closest planet to the Sun. Mercury represents the mind and intelligence. It brings with it influences of communication of all kinds. Mercury rules the astrological signs of Gemini and the energies of communication and education. Also rules Virgo, so brings in energy of an analytical nature.

Venus: The second planet from the Sun. Venus is beauty itself and brings to us the energies of gentleness and grace, and the power of love and quiet persuasion. Venus rules the astrological signs of Taurus and Libra, and serves to be a calming and harmonious aspect of the signs.

Earth: The third planet circling the Sun. This is our home planet and carries the energies of nurturing wisdom, the manifestation of all that is, the grounding element and the fragile balance of all nature and life on this planet.

Mars: The fourth planTu B'Shvat – Sunday, February 8, 2009 at sundown -New Year for the Trees – how to celebrate our connection to the environment and appreciate the fruits of the Land of Israel and share our energies for global wellness. We plant trees and do our part to conserve and unite for a sustainable future.

et from the Sun. It is known as the Red Planet and carries the energies of a physical intensity. It is known as a yang planet (male) as it rules the signs of Aries and Scorpio, which both have courage, assertiveness and determination.

Jupiter: The fifth planet from the Sun. Jupiter is also larger than all the planets put together. It symbolizes higher mind, wisdom and enthusiasm. Jupiter rules the signs Sagittarius and Pisces, and brings with it the desire to improve on all things to expand. Generosity and tolerance also adorn this planet's energy.

Saturn: The sixth planet from the sun, and known as 'the teacher' and 'the wise old man.' It represents justice in the world of cause and effect. Saturn likes form and boundaries, and reminds us that, by facing our responsibilities, we become wiser. Saturn rules the astrological signs of Capricorn and Aquarius.

Uranus: The seventh planet from the Sun. There is a vast space between Saturn and Uranus, its nearest planet. Uranus is the chief ruler of Aquarius.

Neptune is the eighth planet from the Sun and the outermost planet of the gas giants. It has an equatorial diameter of 49,500 kilometers (30,760 miles). That means if Neptune were hollow, it could contain nearly 60 Earths. It takes 165 years for Neptune to complete one orbit around the Sun. Neptune has eight moons, and six of them were discovered by our satellite Voyager. A day on Neptune is just over 16 hours 6.7 minutes. Neptune is considered the higher vibration of Venus. Neptune rules the waters with its deep mysteries and brings deep emotion to beings of this earth. Neptune can be of high spiritual vibration but can also cause a dose of idealistic or escapist energy. Neptune and Jupiter rule the sign of Pisces.

Pluto: The ninth planet from the Sun. This planet is such a great distance away, about 3.67 Billion miles. That is 39 times farther than the earth. It Takes Pluto approximately 248 of our earth years to make one orbit around the Sun. Pluto represents transformation. Death and re birth. Some say it is the sign of spirituality as it dissolves the veils. Pluto may also be the great healer. Pluto rules the sign of Scorpio.

We welcome your comments and questions:
www.openwisdominstitute.com

Bright Blessings to you, Sheila Z

The Seasons and Celebrations

In the ancient ways, these seasonal changes were marked by Festivals and celebrations. Each season of the year being unique to it purpose. "And to every time there is a purpose."

Candlemas: falls on February 2, 2009 in the sign of Aquarius. The energy of Candlemas is that of turning from the dark months towards the spring months. The beginning of the end of winter. Yes, the long winter has come to a waning time and this marks the very first indication of the coming of Spring. (New Light) It is said that this may also have been the beginnings of Groundhog Day.

Vernal or Spring Equinox, aka Ostara— March 20, 2009, (11:47), an event of cosmic proportion. The first day of Aries marks this event. This is one of the two days when light and darkness balance. The cosmic balance. This is the day when you can place an egg on its end and it will stand due to the gravitational pull being equal and balanced. Each day from now on, we add one or two minutes of light to our day until the Summer Solstice in the sign of cancer.

Beltane - May 1, 2009, celebrates the blooming of all mother nature, the full womb of the mother. It is a time of celebration and frolic. Beltane falls on the first of May and is in the sign of Taurus, which, of course, is ruled by Venus. May 1st, also known as *May Day or May Eve*. It announces the union of God and Goddess and the time when the seeds that have been planted now begin to sprout and grow.

Summer Solstice – June 21, 2009. (5:48) The first day of the season of summer is marked by the first day of the astrological sign of Cancer. This cosmic event, the longest day of the year in the Northern Hemisphere, is also called "Leitha" by some as, from this point forward, the days will be getting shorter by about a minute a day, as we make our way towards the Autumn Equinox in the sign of Libra.

Lammas or Lughnasadh: August 1st. This time marks the great harvest, the first harvest. There is always a festival and a great feast. A ripeness and acknowledgment of the caring of the seedlings. A time when many planted seeds are ripe and ready for the feast. This celebration is in the sign of Leo.

Autumn Equinox, aka Mabon, September 22, 2009 at (21:29). This also marks the first day of the sign of Libra, The Equinox signifies the great balance, the beginning of Autumn, the first day of the fall season. The last of the harvest has been reaped and is stored for the coming winter months. This begins the long period of the coming darkness of winter, and all of nature makes ready for the Winter Solstice in the sign of Capricorn.

Samhain: Pronounced "sow-en," it literally means "summer's end." This day marks the time to begin the great reflection, to go within and see what has come to pass, not only in the previous year but of all who have gone before. It is a time when the veils are thin and one may travel between the worlds. And those who have gone before may walk among us. Samhain is on **October 31**, and in the sign of Libra. The great balance between the worlds. Many refer to this as *All Hallows Eve* or *Halloween*. In the ancient ways, this was the New year. The last of the harvest is done, and God and Goddess will rest until the coming spring. It is the Celtic tradition festival held on November 1st this year, which some say marks the Celtic New Year.

Winter Solstice: December 21, 2009 (17:51) the first day of Capricorn, also marks the winter solstice, when the sun is the farthest south. In the Northern Hemisphere, we know this as "the shortest day of the year," the time to enter hibernation, the time of inner transformation. Winter is upon us, but it won't be long before the turning of the wheel, as we look towards the birth of the next spring. Yule is the celebration of the Winter Solstice.

Ancient Remembrances

Tu B'Shvat – Sundown, Sunday, February 8, 2009

New Year for the Trees – We celebrate our connection to the environment and appreciate the fruits of the Land of Israel and share our energies for global wellness. We plant trees and do our part to conserve and unite for a sustainable future. We honor the symbiotic relationship we share with all plant life and the great healing we receive from the trees.

Purim – Monday, March 9 – Tuesday, March 10, 2009

The Holiday of Joy – dress up, drink and be merry while remembering how the Jews of Persia narrowly escaped annihilation thanks to the bravery of Queen Esther

Passover – Sundown, Wednesday April 8, 2009

Celebrates the liberation of the Israelites from slavery in Egypt. A time to remember how the Angel of Death Passed Over those who would be freed from the bondage in Egypt. A time to attain the keys to personal liberation and fulfillment! We gather and share a meal and ask the Four Questions. We taste salt water to remind us of the tears shed in liberation. We eat only unleavened bread (matzah) to remind us of how we fled to be free, not even giving bread a time to rise. This sacred meal is called a Seder and the story of the Exodus is told.

Holocaust Remembrance Day – May 1, 2009

Holocaust Remembrance Day – This is a day of remembrance not only for the 6 million Jews but also for the millions of others who became a part of this time of fallen humanity. It is a time to reflect upon how we as a people of all races, colors and creeds can learn tolerance and learn that we are all one. How we treat each other affects the health and well-being of the entire planet.

Shavuot – Friday, May 29, 2009

This is the day the Torah was given to the Israelites. It celebrates the monumental encounter between God and the Israelites at Mount Sinai, an event that changed mankind forever. Traditionally, the Ten Commandments are read.

The High Holidays

September 18 at sundown – September 20 mark the first two days of Rosh Hashana, and the High Holidays end on Yom Kippur, on Monday, September 28, 2009:

Rosh Hashana – a time when we spiritually "empty our pockets." We gather all that no longer serves to our highest spiritual good and release it to create the empty vessel that is to be filled with divine spirit. A time when we reflect on our lives and think about how we want to be seen by the world in the year to come. It is a time of sweetness, and traditionally apples and honey are eaten to ensure a sweet year.

Yom Kippur – September 28, 2009. The day of atonement, and the culmination of a month-long process of coming back to God. This is the time we may be written into the book of life for the coming year. We honor those who have gone before us and look to a future of connection with spirit.

Chanukah – December 11 (Sundown) – 19, 2009

First candle is lit at sundown December 11, 2009. This holiday is called the miracle of lights, and the rededication of the Temple, when oil meant to last for one day burned for eight, so a candle is lit each night one added each night until the last candle is lit on December 19, 2009. Eight candles in all. Gifts and prayers are offered. It is a joyous holiday and celebration. A time of remembering the miracle of illumination. The miracle of lights.

Reading the Daily Moon Chart

Each day has been divided into three 8-hour sections. Since the cosmos is ever on the move, on some days there will be three signs in one day. On other days, there are two energies in that one day. On the days there is one sign in a day, the Moon is in that sign for that 24-hour period. Many days have the letters V.C., for Void of Course, which means that the moon is in transit between the energies of the signs. This transit usually only lasts a few hours.

Once you see what energies are influencing the day, turn to the page that references that sign to read the formula and about the energies that may be affecting your world on that day.

The moon gently and yet relentlessly reminds us of the cycles not only in celestial bodies but also in our own cycles. To every moment there is a purpose.

The best time to start a business, bring a dream to reality or plan a trip or party is in the first quarter, when the moon is on the rise. The-52 hour period when the moon is coming into its fullness, during the fullness itself and as it begins its waning cycle, the energy of the Cosmos is at its height. As the moon makes its journey into the last quarter, it's a good time for completion, a time of reflection to make ready for the new energies coming in. The night of the dark moon or new moon is the pivotal point in the Language of the Cosmos, representing death and rebirth of the celestial cycle.

Astrological Clock in Prague

NOVEMBER 2008

SUN	MON	TUE	WED	THUR	FRI	SAT
30 Capricorn						1 Sagittarius
2 V.C. Capricorn	3 Capricorn	4 Aquarius	5 Aquarius	6 First Qtr. Aquarius	7 V.C. Pisces	8 Pisces
9 Pisces V.C. Aries	10 Aries	11 V.C. Taurus	12 Taurus	13 Full Moon Taurus V.C. Gemini	14 Gemini	15 V.C. Cancer
16 Cancer	17 Cancer V.C. Leo	18 Leo	19 Last Qtr. V.C. Virgo	20 Virgo	21 Virgo	22 V.C. Libra
23 Libra	24 Libra V.C. Scorpio	25 Scorpio	26 Scorpio V.C. Sagittarius	27 Sagittarius New Moon	28 Sagittarius V.C.	29 Capricorn

DECEMBER 2008

SUN	MON	TUE	WED	THUR	FRI	SAT
	1 Capricorn V.C. Aquarius	2 Aquarius	3 Aquarius V.C.	4 V.C. Pisces	5 Pisces First Qtr.	6 Pisces V.C. Aries
7 Aries	8 Aries V.C. Taurus	9 Taurus	10 Taurus V.C. Gemini	11 Gemini	12 Gemini Full Moon V.C. Cancer	13 Cancer
14 Cancer V.C. Leo	15 Leo	16 Leo V.C.	17 Virgo	18 Virgo	19 Virgo V.C. Libra Last Qtr.	20 Libra
21 Libra V.C. Scorpio	22 Scorpio	23 Scorpio V.C.	24 Sagittarius	25 Sagittarius	26 V.C. Capricorn	27 Capricorn New Moon
28 Capricorn	29 V.C. Aquarius	30 Aquarius	31 V.C. Pisces			

JANUARY 2009

SUN	MON	TUE	WED	THUR	FRI	SAT
				1 Pisces	2 Pisces V.C.	3 Aries
4 Aries First Qtr. V.C.	5 V.C. Taurus	6 Taurus	7 V.C. Gemini	8 Gemini	9 Gemini V.C. Cancer	10 Cancer
11 V.C. Leo Full Moon	12 Leo V.C.	13 Virgo	14 V.C. Libra	15 Virgo V.C. Libra	16 Libra	17 Libra V.C.
18 Scorpio Last Qtr.	19 Scorpio	20 V.C. Sagittarius	21 Sagittarius	22 Sagittarius V.C.	23 Capricorn	24 Capricorn
25 Capricorn V.C. Aquarius	26 Aquarius New Moon	27 Aquarius V.C.	28 Pisces	29 Pisces	30 Pisces Aries	31 Aries

FEBRUARY 2009

SUN	MON	TUE	WED	THUR	FRI	SAT
1 Aries V.C. Taurus	2 Taurus First Qtr.	3 Taurus Gemini	4 Gemini	5 Gemini V.C. Cancer	6 Cancer	7 Cancer V.C. Leo
8 Leo	9 Leo V.C. Full Moon	10 Virgo	11 Virgo V.C.	12 Libra	13 Libra	14 Libra Scorpio
15 Scorpio	16 Scorpio V.C. Sagittarius Last Qtr.	17 Sagittarius	18 Sagittarius V.C.	19 Capricorn	20 Capricorn	21 Capricorn V.C. Aquarius
22 Aquarius	23 Aquarius V.C.	24 Pisces	25 Pisces New Moon	26 Pisces V.C. Aries	27 Aries	28 Aries V.C. Taurus

MARCH 2009

SUN	MON	TUE	WED	THUR	FRI	SAT
1 Taurus	2 Taurus V.C.	3 Gemini	4 First Qtr. Gemini V.C.	5 Cancer	6 Cancer V.C.	7 Leo
8 Leo Virgo	9 Leo Virgo	10 Virgo	11 V.C. Libra Full Moon	12 Libra	13 Libra Scorpio	14 Scorpio
15 Scorpio V.C.	16 Sagittarius	17 Sagittarius	18 Sagittarius V.C. Capricorn Last Qtr.	19 Capricorn	20 Capricorn V.C.	21 Aquarius
22 Aquarius	23 Aquarius V.C. Pisces	24 Pisces	25 Pisces V.C.	26 Aries New Moon	27 Aries V.C.	28 Taurus
29 Taurus	30 Taurus Gemini	31 Gemini				

APRIL 2009

SUN	MON	TUE	WED	THUR	FRI	SAT
			1 Gemini V.C. Cancer	**2** Cancer First Qtr.	**3** Cancer V.C. Leo	**4** Leo
5 Leo V.C. Virgo	**6** Virgo	**7** Virgo V.C. Libra	**8** Libra	**9** Libra Full Moon V.C.	**10** Scorpio	**11** Scorpio
12 Scorpio Sagittarius	**13** Sagittarius	**14** Sagittarius	**15** Capricorn	**16** Capricorn	**17** Capricorn Aquarius Last Qtr.	**18** Aquarius
19 Aquarius V.C.	**20** Pisces	**21** Pisces	**22** Pisces	**23** Pisces Aries	**24** Aries V.C. Taurus	**25** Taurus New Moon
26 Taurus V.C. Gemini	**27** Gemini	**28** Gemini V.C. Cancer	**29** Cancer	**30** Cancer V.C. Leo		

MAY 2009

SUN	MON	TUE	WED	THUR	FRI	SAT
31 Virgo First Qtr.					1 Leo First Qtr.	2 Leo V.C.
3 Virgo	4 Virgo Virgo V.C.	5 Libra	6 Libra	7 Libra Scorpio	8 Scorpio	9 Scorpio V.C. Sagittarius Full Moon
10 Sagittarius	11 Sagittarius	12 Capricorn	13 Capricorn	14 Capricorn V.C. Aquarius	15 Aquarius	16 Aquarius
17 Aquarius Pisces Last Qtr.	18 Pisces	19 Pisces Aries	20 Aries	21 Aries V.C.	22 Taurus	23 Taurus V.C.
24 Gemini New Moon	25 Gemini V.C.	26 Cancer	27 Cancer V.C.	28 Leo	29 Leo	30 Leo Virgo

JUNE 2009

SUN	MON	TUE	WED	THUR	FRI	SAT
	1 Virgo Libra	2 Libra	3 Libra V.C. Scorpio	4 Scorpio	5 Scorpio V.C.	6 Sagittarius
7 Sagittarius Full Moon	8 Sagittarius V.C. Capricorn	9 Capricorn	10 Capricorn V.C.	11 Aquarius	12 Aquarius	13 Aquarius Pisces
14 Pisces	15 Pisces Last Qtr. V.C.	16 Aries	17 Aries	18 Aries Taurus	19 Taurus	20 Taurus Gemini
21 V.C. Gemini Cancer	22 Gemini Cancer New Moon	23 Cancer	24 Cancer Leo	25 Leo	26 Leo Virgo	27 Virgo
28 Virgo V.C. Libra	29 Libra First Qtr.	30 Libra V.C.				

JULY 2009

SUN	MON	TUE	WED	THUR	FRI	SAT
			1 Scorpio	2 Scorpio	3 Scorpio Sagittarius	4 Sagittarius
5 Sagittarius V.C. Capricorn	6 Capricorn	7 Capricorn Full Moon	8 Aquarius	9 Aquarius	10 Aquarius Pisces	11 Pisces
12 Pisces	13 Pisces Aries	14 Aries	15 Aries V.C. Taurus Last Qtr.	16 Taurus	17 Taurus Gemini	18 Gemini
19 Gemini V.C. Cancer	20 Cancer	21 Cancer Leo	22 Leo New Moon	23 Leo V.C. Virgo	24 Virgo	25 Virgo V.C.
26 Libra	27 Libra V.C.	28 Scorpio First Qtr.	29 Scorpio	30 Scorpio V.C. Sagittarius	31 Sagittarius	

AUGUST 2009

SUN	MON	TUE	WED	THUR	FRI	SAT
30 Capricorn	31 Capricorn V.C. Aquarius					1 Sagittarius
2 Capricorn	3 Capricorn	4 Capricorn V.C. Aquarius	5 Aquarius	6 Aquarius Full Moon V.C.	7 Pisces	8 Pisces
9 Pisces V.C. Aries	10 Aries	11 Aries V.C.	12 Taurus	13 Taurus Last Qtr. V.C.	14 Gemini	15 Gemini
16 Cancer	17 Cancer	18 Cancer Leo	19 Leo	20 Leo Virgo New Moon	21 Virgo	22 Virgo Libra
23 Libra	24 Libra Scorpio	25 Scorpio	26 Scorpio V.C. Sagittarius	27 First Qtr.	28 Sagittarius	29 Capricorn

SEPTEMBER 2009

SUN	MON	TUE	WED	THUR	FRI	SAT
		1 Aquarius	2 Aquarius	3 Aquarius Pisces	4 Pisces Full Moon	5 Pisces V.C. Aries
6 Aries	7 Aries V.C.	8 Taurus Gemini	9 Taurus	10 Taurus Gemini	11 Gemini	12 Gemini V.C. Last Qtr. Cancer
13 Cancer	14 Cancer V.C. Leo	15 Leo	16 Leo V.C. Virgo	17 Virgo	18 Virgo Libra New Moon	19 Libra
20 Libra V.C.	21 Scorpio	22 Scorpio	23 Sagittarius	24 Sagittarius	25 Sagittarius V.C. Capricorn	26 Capricorn First Qtr.
27 Capricorn V.C.	28 Aquarius	29 Aquarius	30 Aquarius V.C. Pisces			

OCTOBER 2009

SUN	MON	TUE	WED	THUR	FRI	SAT
				1 Pisces	2 Pisces V.C.	3 Aries
4 Aries Full Moon	5 Taurus	6 Taurus	7 Taurus V.C. Gemini	8 Gemini	9 Gemini Cancer	10 Cancer
11 Cancer Last Qtr. V.C.	12 Leo	13 Leo	14 Virgo	15 Virgo	16 Virgo Libra	17 Libra
18 Libra Scorpio New Moon	19 Scorpio	20 Scorpio Sagittarius	21 Sagittarius	22 Sagittarius	23 Sagittarius Capricorn	24 Capricorn First Qtr.
25 Capricorn Aquarius	26 Aquarius	27 Aquarius	28 Pisces	29 Pisces	30 Pisces Aries	31 Aries

NOVEMBER 2009

SUN	MON	TUE	WED	THUR	FRI	SAT
1 Aries V.C. Taurus	2 Taurus Full Moon	3 Taurus V.C.	4 V.C. Gemini	5 Gemini V.C.	6 Cancer	7 Cancer V.C.
8 Leo	9 Leo V.C.	10 Virgo	11 Virgo Last Qtr.	12 Virgo V.C. Libra	13 Libra	14 Libra V.C. Scorpio
15 Scorpio	16 Scorpio V.C.	17 Sagittarius	18 Sagittarius New Moon V.C.	19 Capricorn	20 Capricorn	21 Capricorn Aquarius
22 Aquarius	23 Aquarius V.C.	24 V.C. Pisces First Qtr.	25 Pisces	26 Pisces V.C. Aries	27 Aries	28 Aries V.C.
29 Taurus	30 Taurus					

DECEMBER 2009

SUN	MON	TUE	WED	THUR	FRI	SAT
		1 Taurus Gemini	2 Gemini Full Moon	3 Gemini Cancer	4 Cancer	5 Cancer V.C. Leo
6 Leo	7 Leo Virgo	8 Virgo	9 Virgo V.C. Libra Last Qtr.	10 Libra	11 Libra V.C. Scorpio	12 Scorpio
13 Scorpio V.C.	14 Sagittarius	15 Sagittarius	16 Sagittarius V.C. Capricorn New Moon	17 Capricorn	18 Capricorn V.C.	19 Aquarius
20 Aquarius	21 Aquarius V.C. Pisces	22 Pisces	23 Pisces V.C.	24 Aries First Qtr.	25 Aries	26 Aries V.C. Taurus
27 Taurus	28 V.C. Gemini	29 Gemini	30 Gemini V.C. Cancer	31 Cancer Full Moon		

Planetary Energy for 2009: Retrograde and Direct Positions

There are times during our yearly planetary cycle that from our vantage point on the Earth, a planet may actually seem to be moving backwards. Planets actually never move backwards; they just appear to. It is an optical illusion. However the perceived energy of the retrograde seems to play havoc with our daily events here on earth. For example when Mercury is in retrograde, and Mercury being the planet of ideas and communication, it is amazing how there may be road blocks or mishaps in your daily life. Also problems with computers, communication, phones, cars seem to increase.

Below is your guide to the planetary positions.

Date	Planetary energy	Degree
Jan 11, 2009	Mercury turns retrograde	07Aqu45
Feb 1, 2009	Mercury turns direct	21Cap44
Mar 6, 2009	Venus turns retrograde	15Ari27
Apr 4, 2009	Pluto turns retrograde	03Cap18
Apr 17, 2009	Venus turns direct	29Pis11
May 7, 2009	Mercury turns retrograde	01Gem44
May 17, 2009	Saturn turns direct	14Vir54
May 29, 2009	Neptune turns retrograde	26Aqu28
May 30, 2009	Mercury turns direct	22Tau52
Jun 15, 2009	Jupiter turns retrograde	27Aqu01
Jul 1, 2009	Uranus turns retrograde	26Pis37
Sep 7, 2009	Mercury turns retrograde	06Lib13
Sep 11, 2009	Pluto turns direct	00Cap39
Sep 29, 2009	Mercury turns direct	21Vir36
Oct 13, 2009	Jupiter turns direct	17Aqu09
Nov 4, 2009	Neptune turns direct	23Aqu41
Dec 1, 2009	Uranus turns direct	22Pis42
Dec 20, 2009	Mars turns retrograde	19Leo41
Dec 26, 2009	Mercury turns retrograde	21Cap47

About the Author

Late in 2006, Sheila was given a transmission that "the race is on." We must now each play our part to raise the vibration of humanity and so raise the frequency of planet Earth. We are in the birth process of the dimensional shift here on earth.

Sheila Z has created an all-day experiential seminar called *Intentional Wellness*™ where you take the journey to activate your future self. It covers a vast array of teachings, from ancient ways to quantum physics. To find out more about this new adventure, please visit the web site: www.intentional-wellness.com.

Sheila Z is a gifted intuitive and a hands-on Healer. Through years of study and working with clients she has become an expert in cosmic energy and how it impacts our lives. As Founder of the Open Wisdom Institute, Sheila facilitates workshops and seminars on Higher Consciousness, Ascension Assistance, Nine Keys to Enlightenment. She is a conscious channel, receiving transmissions of information, music and tones that speak to our souls, and has facilitated accelerated healing for countless individuals. A Reiki Master and Spiritual Advocate, Sheila has an on-going practice in sound healing and is a personal transformation coach. Her meditations have helped countless people find their gifts and their purpose. She facilitates large gatherings, Sacred Ceremony and one-on-one sessions. As a light and energy worker, Sheila walks her talk and has a sincere knowing that we each hold the key to be in divine harmony and that, with this balance, we can heal ourselves, our communities and our planet. She has enriched the lives of many with her insights and grace. Sheila Z is the 2005 recipient of the "Woman of Spirit Award."

Sheila Stirling is the author of *Sounds of the Soul* CD and book, plus *Meditation Miracles, Journey Meditation* and *Sounds of the Soul Healing Meditation* CDs. Sheila is a Spiritual Evolutionist and lives in Las Vegas, Nevada.

January Notes:

February Notes:

March Notes:

April Notes:

May Notes:

June Notes:

July Notes:

August Notes:

September Notes:

October Notes:

November Notes:

December Notes:

Sounds of the Soul CD

Sounds of the Soul was channeled from the celestial realm. Cutting edge scientific studies are now being done with neuro-feedback EEGs and the initial findings are astounding. This CD when listened to through headphones seems to balance Alpha, Beta, Theta, and Delta brain waves. The implications of this are boundless and, as we know, meditation has the ability to decrease blood pressure and stress levels. We also know that *Sounds of the Soul* may potentially normalize brain function and, in doing so, heal the body on a cellular and soul level. Open your heart and breathe in the music.

Sounds of the Soul was channeled through Sheila Z in collaboration with Gary Stadler of Heartmagic Studios, and is an interpretation of the God code of creation. The sounds and tones are very relaxing and channel directly to the soul. Many have experienced a reconnection with spirit and accelerated healing.

There are 2 tracks on this CD. One is 18:50 min and the other is 27:24 minutes.

To order, please go to: www.openwisdominstitute.com. Click on Books & CDs, or Store, and listen to a free clip of the CD. $15 plus $5 shipping within the United States.

Journey Meditation CD

This CD has two meditations on it. The first is a grounding and centering meditation and followed by a healing journey meditation.
The total time of this CD is about 25 minutes.

**To order, go to: www.openwisdominstitute.com and order online.
$15 plus $5 shipping within the United States.**

Healing Meditation with the Sounds of the Soul CD

This is a journey meditation that encourages your connection to the healer within. Building the healing energy of the cosmos an being in the heightened vibrations of the angelic realms from Sounds of the Soul.
This meditation is about 27 minutes.

To order or comment, please go to the web site: www.openwisdominstitute.com.
$19.95 plus $5 shipping within the United States.

Printed in the United States
130809LV00004B/103-150/P